The Legal Terms Common to the Macedonian Inscriptions and the New Testament

The Legal Terms Common to the Macedonian Inscriptions and the New Testament

By
WILLIAM DUNCAN FERGUSON, PH.D.

WIPF & STOCK · Eugene, Oregon

Wipf and Stock Publishers
199 W 8th Ave, Suite 3
Eugene, OR 97401

The Legal Terms Common to the Macedonian Inscriptions and the New Testament
By Ferguson, William Duncan
ISBN 13: 978-1-60608-380-2
Publication date 01/05/2009
Previously published by University of Chicago, 1913

INTRODUCTION

The inscriptions upon which this treatise is based are the Greek Macedonian inscriptions. Thus far the Corpus does not contain all of the Macedonian inscriptions. Dimitsas, having spent ten years in making a collection of these inscriptions, published them in Athens, in 1896, in two volumes entitled, Ἡ Μακεδονία. In this work Dimitsas has included all inscriptions having any reference to Macedonian affairs, regardless of the place to which the inscription itself belonged. For our present purpose we make use of only those inscriptions which had their origin in Macedonia, that is, only those which are geographically Macedonian inscriptions.

This treatise is intended to present an inductive study of the legal and governmental terms common to the Macedonian inscriptions and the New Testament. The purpose of this investigation is to obtain, from the usage of these words in the inscriptions, any available information which may throw light upon their interpretation in the New Testament. The object is not to make an exhaustive investigation of the meaning and usage of these words in the whole field of Greek literature, nor yet to carry the investigation into the New Testament itself, but rather to furnish to the student of the New Testament some additional data with which to approach his task of interpreting these technical terms in the Scriptures.

The method has been to quote in Greek the statement in which the word under consideration occurs; to indicate to what time and place the inscription belonged; to give a translation or a paraphrase of a sufficient portion of the immediate context to enable the reader to understand the shorter passage quoted in Greek; and then to make an inductive study of the terms selected, in every inscription in which they occur.

Arabic numerals, unless otherwise specified, refer to the numbers assigned to the Macedonian inscriptions by Dimitsas in his Μακεδονία, and the Roman numerals refer to the divisions of this treatise. Under each Roman numeral a single word, or group of closely related words, is treated. The abbreviations used for names of authors are usually from the list given by Liddell and Scott.

I wish to make special mention of my indebtedness to Professor Ernest D. Burton of the University of Chicago. His discriminating and suggestive criticisms, so generously given, greatly stimulated my interest and gave direction to my effort. His help has been so many-sided that it is impossible to estimate its value. To Professor Edgar Goodspeed of the University of Chicago I also desire to express my thanks and grateful appreciation for his pertinent suggestions on various linguistic problems.

TABLE OF CONTENTS

BIBLIOGRAPHY

Archäologische Zeitung. Berlin, 1880, pp. 159–61.

Boeckh, *Corpus Inscriptionum Graecarum.* Berlin, 1828–1877.

Bonner, *Evidence in Athenian Courts.* Chicago, 1905.

Buck, *Greek Dialects.* Boston, 1910.

Burton, *The Politarchs in Macedonia and Elsewhere.* Chicago, 1898.

Corpus Inscriptionum Atticarum.

Cousinéry, *Voyage dans la Macédoine.* Paris, 1831.

Deissmann, *Bible Studies.* Edinburgh, 1901.

Dittenberger, *Orientis Graeci Inscriptiones selectae,* Vols. I, II. Leipzig, 1903–1905.

Dittenberger, *Sylloge Inscriptionum Graecarum.* Leipzig, 1883.

Dumont, *Éphébie Attique.* 2 vols. Paris, 1875, 1876.

Gardner and Jevons, *Manual of Greek Antiquities.* New York, 1895.

Gilbert, *Constitutional Antiquities of Sparta and Athens.* London and New York, 1895.

Goodspeed, *Greek Papyri from the Cairo Museum.* Chicago, 1903.

Goodspeed, *Index Patristicus.* Leipzig, 1907.

Grenfell and Hunt, *Oxyrhynchus Papyri,* Vols. I–IV. London, 1898–1904.

Hatch, *Essays in Biblical Greek.* Oxford, 1889.

Herwerden, *Lexicon Graecum Suppletorium et Dialecticum.* 1902.

Hicks and Hill, *Greek Historical Inscriptions.* Oxford, 1901.

Josephus, *De Bello Judaico.*

Journal of Hellenic Studies, VIII, 1887, 284, 362–63, 424–26.

Kaibel, *Epigrammata Graeca ex Lapidibus Conlecta.* Berlin, 1878.

Kennedy, *Sources of N. T. Greek.* Edinburgh, 1895.

King, *Demosthenes, The Oration against Leptines.* London, 1881.

Le Bas et Waddington, *Voyage en Grèce et en Asie Mineure,* Vols. II, III. Paris, 1848.

Müller, K. O., *Die Dorier,* Vols. I, II. Breslau, 1844.

Norton, *A Lexicographical and Historical Study of διαθήκη.* Chicago, 1908.

Pape, *Wörterbuch der griechischen Eigennamen.* 2 vols. Leipzig, 1884.

Ramsay, *Paul's Epistle to the Galatians.* New York, 1900.

Roberts, *Introduction to Greek Epigraphy.* Cambridge, 1887.

Schürer, *The Jewish People in the Time of Jesus Christ.* New York, 1891.

Searles, *Lexicographical Study of the Greek Inscriptions.* Chicago, 1898.

Thumb, *Die Griechische Sprache im Zeitalter des Hellenismus.* Strassburg, 1901.

Thumb, *Handbuch der Griechischen Dialekte.* Heidelberg, 1909.

Westcott and Hort, *The New Testament in the Original Greek,* Vol. II. New York, 1898.

I. A.   βουλή

(1)

1

Ἀγαθῇ τύχῃ,
ἔτους η̅κτ̅ ἀπογραφὴ
ἐφήβων τῶν ἐφηβευσάν-
των ὑπὸ Λυσίμαχον Ἀβι-
5   διανοῦ τὸν ἐφήβαρχον
κατὰ τὸ δόγμα τῆς βουλῆς.

The whole of this inscription is extant, and the first six lines are here transcribed. It reads as follows: "In the year 328 a register of the ἔφηβοι who became ἔφηβοι under Lysimachus the son of Abidianos the ἐφήβαρχος by the decree of the βουλή." Then follows a list of the ἔφηβοι.

This inscription was found over the entrance of the city of Bodena (Edessa). Edessa was situated on a table-land between two projections of the Bermius Mountains, and was at one time the capital of Macedonia.

Boeckh, reckoning the date found in the inscription (l. 2) from the destruction of Corinth, gives us the year 182 A.D. as the date of this inscription.

It here appears that the boys who became ἔφηβοι were under the control of an officer called ὁ ἐφήβαρχος, and they were duly registered as ἔφηβοι by a decree of the βουλή (cf. *CIG*, 256, 272B, 275, 276, Heliod. 7, 8). The βουλή is the only official body here mentioned, and it had authority to confer the rights of citizenship upon the youths of the city. This may indicate that in some of the Macedonian cities there was only one governing body in the city, as in the case of the Sanhedrin in Jerusalem, or it may be that this particular matter, the granting of citizenship to the young men was one which pertained to the functions of the βουλή.

(2)   37

ἀλλ' ἐλέησον ἡμᾶς ὡς
5   υἱο(ὺ)ς αὐτοῦ πρεσβ[ε]ίαις καὶ εὐχαῖς π[άντων?
ἀγγέλων [καὶ] προφητῶν ἀπο . .
μαρτύρων τοῖς σοὶ ἀρέσασ(ι)
. . . . . βουλῆς κόσμου ἀμήν.

227]   11

'Ενθάδε κεῖτε 'Ιωαννήσκη τοῦ το—

10   . . . . ἀ]ναπαυσαμένη ἐν Χριστῷ.

The whole of this mortuary inscription is extant except for slight
mutilations. It is here transcribed from the middle of l. 4 to the end
of the inscription. It was placed on the monument of a certain Cyprian
whose tomb had been destroyed during a persecution of the Christians,
and the part quoted above is in the form of a prayer by those who
erected the monument and who in some sense regarded themselves
as his sons. It reads thus: "but have mercy upon us as his sons because
of the supplications and prayers of all the angels and of the prophets
and of the witnesses to those things which are pleasing to thee, [and
deliver us from (καὶ ῥῦσαι ἡμᾶς ἀπὸ)] the counsel of the world. Amen."
This inscription was found in the outer wall of a church in Bodena.
Its exact date is not known, but the phrase, ἀναπαυσαμένη ἐν Χριστῷ,
marks it as belonging to the Christian era.

Since the last part of l. 6 and the first part of l. 8 are wanting, the
exact relationship of the phrase, βουλῆς κόσμου ἀμήν, to the context
cannot be determined with certainty. In the New Testament the
word βουλή almost invariably means "counsel," and κόσμος frequently
denotes "men," or "the ungodly multitude." That the inscription
is of a religious character is evident. The opening words of the sentence
beginning on l. 4, ἐλέησον ἡμᾶς, are used at the present time in the
liturgy of the Greek church. The ἀμήν at the close of the sentence
is the word commonly employed in ending a prayer. The thought
expressed is that of petition or prayer. It thus appears that βουλῆς
is here used in the closing phrase of a prayer, and that it is an abstract
term having a usage parallel to that found in the New Testament.
In Luke 7:30, τὴν βουλὴν τοῦ θεοῦ denotes the counsel of God (cf.
Acts 2:23; 20:27, etc.). The βουλή in the inscription pretty certainly
denotes counsel, and probably κόσμος denotes the ungodly people.
According to this interpretation there seems to be a contrast between
the prayers and supplications of the angels and of the prophets on the
one hand, and the counsel of the world on the other.

(3)   50
            'Η βουλὴ καὶ [ὁ δῆμος] Ποπίλιον
            Σούμμον νεώτερον.

The whole of this inscription is extant and is here transcribed. It
was found in the ruins of an old wall in Beroea, a city of Macedonia

lying about seven hours south of Edessa, and twelve west of Thessalonica. The date is not known, but the Latin name, Ποπίλιος Σούμμος,
points to the Roman period. The two following inscriptions (51, 52)
belong to the same place, and probably to about the same time.
In monumental inscriptions the name of the person or persons
erecting the monument, and the name of the person for whom it was
erected are usually given, while the verb of erecting or setting up is
often omitted. It here appears that the βουλή and the δῆμος erected
a monument to Ποπίλιος Σούμμος νεώτερος. The term βουλή is used in
its technical sense referring to a civil body, the council of the city.

(4)   51
                        Ἡ βουλὴ καὶ οἱ νέοι
                        Κ. Ποπίλλιον Πρόκλον Ἰουνια-
                        νὸν Πύθωνα τὸν γυμνασίαρχον
                        ἀλείψαντα καὶ λούσαντα δι’ ὅλης
5   ἡμέρας πανδημεί.

The whole of this inscription is extant, and is here transcribed.
For place and date see I. A. (3). It reads as follows: "The Council
and the boys erect this monument to C. Popillius Proclus Junianus
Python the gymnasiarch who spent his time anointing and bathing
the boys throughout the whole day."
It is to be observed that the βουλή and the νέοι are represented
as acting together in erecting a monument in honor of the gymnasiarch.
This is the only instance in the Macedonian inscriptions in which the
βουλή and the νέοι are thus associated. Elsewhere, such official
action is always attributed either to ἡ βουλή καὶ ὁ δῆμος, or to either
one of these bodies acting by itself. In this case, however, the boys
share with the βουλή in honoring the gymnasiarch, because in his
official capacity as superintendent of the gymnasia he had devoted
all his time to caring for the boys. This does not indicate that the
νέοι had a political standing.

(5)   52
                        Βεροια[ί]ων ἡ βουλὴ καὶ ὁ [δῆμος]
                        Τι . . . . αιον Πτολεμαῖον
                        . . . . την τῶν σεβαστῶν

This inscription is in a badly mutilated condition, and is here transcribed. It was found in a church in Beroea. It appears that the βουλή

and the δῆμος erected a monument in honor of the person whose name is partly obliterated in l. 2. It is expressly stated that this is the βουλή of the Beroeans. In Nos. 50 and 52 δῆμος has been restored by the editor. In No. 50 it may have been originally ἡ βουλὴ καὶ οἱ νέοι, as in 51:1, and in 52:1 there is also the possibility of such a restoration as νέοι. These are the only inscriptions found in Beroea in which the βουλή is mentioned, and in each case it is used in a technical sense, denoting a political body. The only unusual feature in its usage is its association with the νέοι in 51:1.

(6) 258

10 κ(αὶ) τελευτῶν οὐδὲ τῆς
  κατὰ τὴν βουλὴν τε(ι)μῆς ἠμέλησεν,

. . . .

16 ἔδοξεν τῇ βουλῇ
  τὴν τοῦ ἀνδρὸς σεμνότητα κ(αὶ) βούλησιν
  ἀποδέξεσθαι

. . . .

  ὁ ἐπιμελη-
26 τὴς τῶν τῆς βουλῆς δηναρίων Λούκιος
  Λουκρήτιος Πούδης.

The whole of this inscription is extant, but only those clauses are here transcribed which contain the term βουλή. It was found at Tzepikobon, a small town about five hours from Bitolia in Pelagonia, and about one hundred and thirty-seven miles from Thessalonica. The date (243) contained in the inscription if reckoned from the Achaean era (146 B.C.) corresponds to 97 A.D.

Beginning at the middle of l. 9, the inscription runs thus: "Inasmuch as Philo both greatly honored his own native land, and when dying lacked nothing of honor toward the βουλή, but left to it, by will, 1,500 denarii on the condition that from the interest accruing from it annually the Council should celebrate a festive day in honor of Οὐέττιος Βωλανός to be held on the fourteenth day before the Calends of November, it is decreed by the βουλή to accept the offer of Philo in the proposed conditions written by him in the will, to receive the money, and, from the interest on it, to celebrate annually the festal day, and not to spend any of the principal for other need, nor to spend any of the interest except as Philo who gave it had planned. The money was counted and the curator of the βουλή received it."

Since the δῆμος is not mentioned in this inscription, it may be inferred either that the βουλή was the only governmental body in Tzepikobon, or that the matter in question—that of accepting a bequest—was one which belonged to the functions of the βουλή apart from the δῆμος. Coming, as it does, at the close of the first century A.D., it is of first-rate importance in determining the authority of the βουλή in this part of Macedonia during the New Testament period.

It is seen that at Tzepikobon at this time:

a) The πολιτάρχαι convened the council (ll. 5–6).

b) That money might be left by will (κατὰ διαθήκην) to the βουλή to be expended for public purposes as directed by the testator.

c) That the βουλή had authority to accept such a bequest and to carry out the required conditions.

d) The βουλή had an officer who took charge of money committed to it.

(7)   365

8   κατὰ τὰ γενόμενα ὑπὸ τῆς κρατίσ-

9   [της βουλ]ῆς καὶ τοῦ δήμου ψηφίσματα.

Only a part of this inscription is preserved, and the part which is found is in a very fragmentary condition. A part of ll. 8 and 9 is here transcribed. It was found in Thessalonica, and contains its own date, 289 (l. 14), which corresponds to 143 A.D.

The name of the person who is referred to as having left to the city of Thessalonica a legacy is partly defaced so that editors differ as to whether it is the name of a man or of a woman. According to the restoration of Dimitsas it was a woman who made the bequest (ll. 5–6), but according to Hogarth it was a man (*Jour. Hell. Studies*, VIII, 1887, 363).

The inscription as we possess it is so fragmentary that it is hardly safe to venture on a translation of it. Hogarth says: "It is too fragmentary to do more than conjecture that it refers to certain hunting-grounds left by the will of one Herennius, either to the city of Thessalonica or to some religious foundation therein, and the object of the inscription would seem to be to record the terms of their future regulation" (*Jour. Hell. Studies*, VIII, 1887, 362). In addition to this statement it is seen that these games were to be conducted, according to the terms decreed by the βουλή and the δῆμος, by those who were politarchs. Then follow the names of the politarchs, the time of the year at which the games were to be held, and the date of the inscription.

In Tzepikobon it is the βουλή alone which is represented as receiving money through a bequest. Here it is the βουλή and the δῆμος acting together who accept the money and direct the use of it according to the terms of the διαθήκη. This tends to show that the cities of Macedonia did not have a uniform political system. There is a difference of forty-six years in the dates of these two inscriptions (258 and 365), but when compared with other inscriptions, some of an earlier and some of a later date, it is seen that the difference in time will not account for the fact that at Tzepikobon there is only one political body mentioned, while at Thessalonica there are two, the βουλή and the δῆμος, exercising precisely the same functions as those of the βουλή at Tzepikobon. The terms σύνκλητος (1. 5) and βουλή (1. 9) are used interchangeably.

(8)   668

5   ᾿Αλλαι μὲν βουλαὶ ἀνθρώπων,
                 ἄλλα δὲ θεὸς κελεύει.

The whole of this inscription is extant, and the last two lines are here transcribed. It was found in a church in Thessalonica, and bears the date 1705 A.D. It is apparently an inscription of dedication at a time when the church was repaired or rebuilt. It is stated in the nscription that these things took place at the departure of the most holy Ignatius from the island of Lesbos. The two lines which are transcribed seem to be in the form of a proverb: "Men counsel one thing, but otherwise God commands."

The use of βουλή here is of value solely as showing what modern Greek usage is. It has the same meaning as that which it usually has in the New Testament, "counsel" or "purpose."

(9)   671

1   ᾿Εδοξεν τῆι βουλῆι καὶ τῶι δήμωι.

.   .   .   .

8   δεδόχθαι τῆι βουλῆι καὶ τῶι δήμωι.

.   .   .   .

17   ἀναγράψαι δὲ τόδε τὸ ψήφισμα τὴν
                 βουλὴν εἰς τὸ βουλευτήριον.

.   .   .   .

20   ᾿Εδοξεν τῆι βουλῆι καὶ τῶι δήμωι

.   .   .   .

232

27   δεδόχθαι τῆι βουλῆι καὶ τῶι δήμωι

        .   .   .   .

        Ἡ πόλις Θεσσαλονικέων Δηλίων τῆι
46   βουλῆι καὶ τῶι δήμωι χαίρειν.

The whole of this inscription is extant, but only those portions of it
are here transcribed in which the term (βουλή) under consideration
at this point occurs. It was found in Delos in 1885, and contains three
decrees. According to Dimitsas (Μακ., I, 565), it belongs within the
period 220–215 B.C.

FIRST DECREE

Because of the completeness and importance of this inscription,
and inasmuch as it affords a good illustration of the form and character
of many of these inscriptions, a translation of the whole of it is here
appended: "It is decreed by the βουλή and the δῆμος; Boulon the son
of Tunnon made the motion. Since Admetos while a πρόξενος (at
Delos) supplied many great necessaries to the temple and to the Delians,
both publicly and privately, always to whoever of the citizens chanced
to meet him, and in order therefore that the δῆμος appear grateful to
as many as honor the temple, and have been publicly announced as
showing kindness to the βουλή of Delos; be it decreed by the βουλή
and the δῆμος to honor him with the sacred crown of laurel and with
two bronze images, and that the sacred herald proclaim him publicly
in the theater during the sacrifices to Apollo, and whenever the choruses
of boys contend let proclamation be made; and let the δῆμος of Delos
adorn Admetos Bokros a Macedonian with the sacred crown of laurel
and with two bronze images on account of his reverence toward the
temple and of his good-will toward the δῆμος of Delos, and let the βουλή
inscribe this decree in the council chamber, and let the sacred officers
inscribe it in the temple. Cynthiades the son of Teleson put it to the
vote."

SECOND DECREE

"It is decreed by the βουλή and the δῆμος. Boulon the son of
Tunnon made the motion. Since Admetos the πρόξενος supplied
many great needs to the temple and the δῆμος of Delos, both publicly
and privately, always, to whoever of the citizens chanced to meet him;
and in order therefore that the δῆμος appear grateful, to as many as
honor the temple and have been proclaimed for showing them kindness;
with good luck, be it decreed by the βουλή and the δῆμος to set up two

bronze images of the πρόξενος Admetos, the one in the temple and the
other in Thessalonica, and to set the one in the temple beside the altar
of the god of the city, and to inscribe upon the image this inscription;
'The δῆμος of Delos erects this to Admetos the son of Bokros a Macedonian, on account of his valor and of his piety toward the temple and
of his good-will for the δῆμος of Delos;' and to send an envoy who
when he arrives at Thessalonica shall hand over the decrees, and shall
require the δῆμος of Thessalonica, since it is a friend and kindred of
the δῆμος of Delos, to give a place as good as possible for the setting up
of the crown and of the image of Admetos, containing the same inscription which the δῆμος set up also in Delos, and doing these things they
will show gratitude to the δῆμος of Delos. Cynthiades the son of
Teleson put it to the vote. Boulon the son of Tunnon was chosen
envoy."

THIRD DECREE

"The city of Thessalonica to the βουλή and the δῆμος of Delos
greeting. Boulon who was sent an envoy by you, having arrived and
having delivered over the decrees by means of which you honored
Admetos the son of Bokros, and having come into the ἐκκλησία, and
making a speech in accordance with the things decreed, we accepted
these things in accordance with your wish, and of the decree in which
we submitted to the demand made by you we have sent you the copy
just as you see it. Sosipater the president, and the . . . . Menander,
Nicodemos, Philodemos, Hippias . . . . made a motion. Since Boulon
who was sent by the δῆμος of Delos an envoy to the city (Thessalonica)
delivered up the decrees in which the δῆμος, having advised to render
thanks to Admetos the son of Bokros on account of his good deeds,
has adorned him with the divine crown of laurel and with two bronze
images of which it was voted to place one in the sacred place beside
the altar of the god of the city, and to place the other in Thessalonica,
and the inscribing of the crown and the setting up of the image shall
be executed just as it was written in the inscription by the decree, and
they esteemed our city worthy affectionately to give to him as good a
place as possible both in accordance with the things decreed and with
the speech of Boulon; be it decreed by the βουλή, to commend the
δῆμος of Delos, because it gave thanks to the Thessalonian fellow-
citizens of Admetos when it crowned him on account of the good deeds
mentioned, esteeming him worthy of the things decreed, and be it decreed
that the one presiding over the contests pay for the inscribing of the

crown and for the setting up of the image on whatever place seemed best to the members of the βουλή."

The first decree (ll. 1–19) was passed by the βουλή and the δῆμος of Delos in honor of Admetos of Thessalonica who was a πρόξενος at Delos. On account of his benefactions to the temple and to the people of Delos it was decreed by the βουλή and the δῆμος that the herald should proclaim him in the theater during the games, and crown him with the sacred crown of laurel, and the βουλή was to inscribe this decree in their council chamber, and the temple officers were to inscribe it in the temple.

The second decree (ll. 20–45) is similar to the first, with two additions, the one concerning the placing of one of the images of Admetos in the temple beside the altar of Zeus, and the other referring to the choosing of Boulon to go as an envoy to Thessalonica with this decree.

The third decree (ll. 46–77) pertains to the receiving of the envoy from Delos by the ἐκκλησία of Thessalonica, and the reply of Thessalonica to Delos. It relates that Boulon the envoy from Delos had been received at a meeting of the ἐκκλησία, and that in a speech before that body he had presented to them the request of Delos that they also share in honoring Admetos. His plea was favorably received by the βουλή of Thessalonica, and they decreed that one of the bronze images of Admetos should be set up in Thessalonica, and that the crown be inscribed, in accordance with the request of Delos.

It is seen from this inscription:

a) That both of these cities, Delos and Thessalonica, possessed a βουλή and a δῆμος.

b) That the βουλή and the δῆμος of Delos passed a decree honoring the πρόξενος from Thessalonica for the services he had rendered to Delos.

c) That upon the βουλή and the δῆμος devolved the duty and the right to decide where the decree should be inscribed, and the statues set up.

d) That official matters between two cities were transacted by the βουλή and the δῆμος of the respective cities, through the agency of an envoy (πρεσβευτής).

e) That the man chosen as envoy was also a member of the βουλή.

f) That the βουλή of Thessalonica took the initiative and recommended to the δῆμος that Admetos should be honored, but that the final authority in dealing with the matter rested with the δῆμος.

235

(10)   675

36   δεδόχθαι Ληταίων τῆι βουλῆι καὶ τῶι δήμωι

The whole of this inscription is extant, but only the clause in which
the term βουλή occurs is here transcribed. It was inscribed on a large
stone slab, and was found in the village of Aivati, a small town four
hours north of Thessalonica, in Mygdonia. The date contained in the
inscription (l. 49) corresponds to 117 B.C.

The inscription records that the politarchs of the city of Lete, in
a προβούλευμα, proclaimed the Roman treasurer Marcus Annius a
benefactor of Macedonia and of their own city, and they erected to
his honor a stone slab in the market-place on which they placed this
inscription, because he had twice fought with them against hostile
invaders, and had in each case defeated the enemy. For this double
victory the βουλή and the δῆμος voted to crown him, and to establish
in his honor a cavalry contest to be held once a year. Beginning at
the middle of l. 36 it reads as follows: "Because of which be it decreed
by the βουλή and by the δῆμος to praise Marcus Annius the son of
Poplius, the Roman treasurer, and to crown him with the olive wreath,
and to establish for him a cavalry contest, in the month of Δαίσιος."

It appears that at this time Lete had local self-government, and that
here, as well as in Thessalonica, there were two political bodies, a
βουλή and a δῆμος.

As to the relation of the βουλή to the δῆμος, and their method of
conducting business, it is seen that the βουλή took the initiative (671:70,
675:2–3). The βουλή first held a meeting by itself, in which it took
any matter of business under its own consideration and formulated
a statement regarding it, which was then presented to the δῆμος at a
joint meeting of the βουλή and the δῆμος. This preliminary statement
was drawn up in the form of a resolution, and was called a προβούλευμα,
and if approved by a vote of the δῆμος it became an authoritative
decree. At Lete this προβούλευμα was presented to the δῆμος by the
πολιτάρχαι, a variation from the usage of Athens where the office of
πολιτάρχης did not exist. In Athens the προβούλευμα was usually
presented to the δῆμος by the herald, and defended before the assembly
(ἐκκλησία, the joint meeting of the βουλή and the δῆμος) by the man
who first made the motion in the βουλή (Cf. Gilbert, *Greek Const. Ant.*,
pp. 293–96).

The βουλή and the δῆμος voted to grant certain honors to Marcus
Annius, the Roman treasurer, and to choose three envoys (πρεσβευταί)

from among the βουλευταί (l. 49), who should convey to Marcus
Annius the proposal of the δῆμος to honor him, and to urge upon him
the acceptance of these honors. They also provided for the writing and
the setting-up of this decree in a public place. In this case the writing
of the decree and the setting-up of the stele were to be in the hands of
the πολιτάρχαι and of the treasurer of the city. Lete had its own
local treasurer, and the jurisdiction of the Roman treasurer seems to
have extended over matters of general interest, rather than to matters
of the local city government.

(11)   1130
3   κατὰ ψήφισμα βουλῆς καὶ δήμου

　　　．　　．　　．　　．　　．　　．　　．
5   δεδόχθαι τῆι βουλῆι καὶ τῷ δήμῳ

The whole of this inscription is extant, and the two clauses in which
the term βουλή occurs are transcribed. It was found at Thasos. The
exact date to which it belongs is not known, but according to Perrot
it is to be assigned to the period immediately preceding the time of
Alexander the Great (Dim., Мак. II, p. 856).

It is a decree passed by the βουλή and the δῆμος of Thasos praising
a certain Poluaretos and granting to him the rights of citizenship
because of his benefactions to the city of Thasos, and to the people
privately, while he was πρόξενος at Thasos.

Beginning on l. 2 it reads thus: "The θεῦροί made the inscription
according to the decree of the βουλή and the δῆμος. With good luck;
since Polyaretos the son of Hystias, being a πρόξενος and a benefactor
of the city, has been a good man toward the city of Thasos, and does
whatever good he can, both publicly to the city and privately to whoever
chances to meet him; be it decreed by the βουλή and the δῆμος to
praise Polyaretos the son of Hystias on account of his valor and of his
good-will toward the city of Thasos, and that Polyaretos be a citizen,"
etc.

It appears from this inscription that Thasos had a βουλή and a
δῆμος, three ἄρχοντες (l. 1), and three θεῦροί who inscribed this decree
(ll. 2, 10).

(12)   1140
Σῶμα κόρης ἁρπαχθὲν ἀνηλίκῳ εὐθαλεῖ ὥρῃ
παρθένου ἀνθοφόρου τύμβος ὅδ' ἐγκατέχει.
ψυχὴ δ' ἀθανάτων βουλαῖς ἐπιδήμιός ἐστιν
ἄστροις, καὶ ἱερὸν χῶρον ἔχει μακάριον.

The whole of this mortuary inscription is extant. The first four
lines are here transcribed. It was found in Thasos. The date has
not been determined. The contrast between body and soul which
occurs here (ll. 1–3) is found as early as Plato (*Tim.* 42b–d). A translation of the portion which is transcribed is as follows: "This tomb
contains within it the body of a girl, a flower-bearing virgin, snatched
away in the tender bloom of immaturity. But the soul by the counsels of
the immortals is sojourning in the stars, and has a sacred, happy abode."

Liddell and Scott refer to this inscription under the word ἀνθοφόρος
which they interpret as denoting a flower-bearer in a religious rite.
There is a contrast between σῶμα (l.1) and ψυχή (l.3). The contrast
is not only between the σῶμα and the ψυχή, but also between their places
of abode. The tomb holds the body of the maid, but her soul, by the
counsels of the immortals, is sojourning (ἐπιδήμιος; cf. *Ap. Rh.*,
I, 827) among the stars, and has a sacred, happy abode. It thus appears
that this inscription is of a religious character, and that it discloses to
us the conception of the writers as to the existence of the soul after it
has left the body.

As the term βουλή is here used it evidently means counsels, and is
used in an abstract rather than a concrete sense. The latter is usual in
the inscriptions. The usage of βουλή in this inscription is of significance
in its bearing upon its usage in the New Testament, because it is here
used in the abstract sense with a meaning similar to that which it has
in the New Testament, and because there is a certain influence or
authority attributed to the counsels (βουλαί) of the immortals. A
similar conception meets us in the New Testament, where seven out
of the thirteen occurrences of βουλή are used of the counsel of God, and
to the counsel of God is ascribed an authority similar to that which
it has in the inscription. The βουλή of God has an ethical value, and
expresses an ethical principle, or standard of conduct for man. In
Luke 7:30 the νομικοί are regarded as making a wrong choice morally
when they set aside the βουλή of God. In the inscription the βουλαί
of the immortals are associated with the welfare of a soul, and determine its place of abode. The βουλαί of the immortals and the βουλή
of God are both related to the well-being of the soul.

(13)   1141
2   κατ[ὰ] ψήφισμα [βουλῆς καὶ δήμου.

Only a fragment of this inscription is preserved. There is not one
complete line of the original inscription left. The restoration of βουλή

in the line transcribed rests on good authority; it is supported by comparison with other inscriptions. We are, however, not dependent upon this restoration for the fact that there was a βουλή at Thasos where this inscription was found.

(14)   1369

21   καὶ ὁμόσαι τοῦ δ]ήμου ὅν ἄν ἡ βουλή συγγράφῃ

Only a part of this inscription is found. There is no means of telling how much of it has been lost, but only the latter portion of it now remains. There is but one occurrence of the term βουλή in the extant part of it. It was found at Thasos where it had been built into the wall of a Byzantine church, and belongs to the year 411 B.C. It records the revolutionary action of the oligarchical party which in that year attempted, and for a time successfully, to overthrow the government of the δῆμος (Thucyd. VIII).

It appears from this inscription that:

a) The oligarchy canceled all special privileges formerly granted by the δῆμος (ll. 1–4).

b) Rewards were voted to those who had assisted in the revolution (ll. 4–5).

c) The oligarchy restored to civic rights all those who had been exiled by the δῆμος (ll. 5–9).

d) It promised certain honors and immunities to anyone who would contribute money to the city (ll. 9–12).

e) Provision was made in this decree against a counter-revolution by voting that this decree was to be permanent.

f) This decree was to be inscribed and set up in a public place (ll. 16–17).

g) Copies of the decree were to be inscribed and preserved (ll. 17–19).

h) An oath of allegiance to the new government was demanded (ll. 19–21). The line transcribed above reads: "And whomever of the δῆμος the βουλή write down shall take the oath." The δῆμος here referred to (l. 21) was a nominal body of five thousand, created by the oligarchy, but without any active part in the government. It must not be confounded with the δῆμος mentioned in l. 2, whose authority was for a time set aside by the oligarchy.

The term βουλή is here used with reference to the oligarchy, and does not have the same connotation as in the other Macedonian inscriptions. This body which is here called a βουλή was opposed to the

239

democratic principles of government for which the βουλή and the δῆμος of other Macedonian cities stood. It appears, therefore, that the term βουλή does not always carry with it a reference to the kind of organization for which it stands. It may be applied to political bodies representing fundamentally different conceptions of government. This fact may be of importance in considering the different names by which Josephus designates the Sanhedrin of Jerusalem.

In the Macedonian inscriptions the word βουλή, or some form of it, is found in fourteen inscriptions, and in these it occurs twenty-two times. In addition to this, the word βουλευτής, which occurs in 744:1, indicates the existence of a βουλή at Olynthus. In two of these inscriptions (668:5; 1140:3) the plural number occurs with the meaning of counsels or plans, and in 37:8 the singular number of the noun is found, in a prayer, with the same meaning. In every other occurrence of the word in the inscriptions it is used in its technical sense denoting one of the civil bodies commonly found in these Macedonian cities, Edessa (1, 37), Beroea (50, 51, 52), Tzepikobon (258), Thessalonica (365, 668), Lete (675), Olynthus (744), and in two other cities which Dimitsas designates as Macedonian, Delos (671) and Thasos (1130, 1140, 1141, 1369).

The time covered by these inscriptions which refer to the βουλή extends from the latter part of the fifth century B.C. to the end of the second century A.D., and probably later in several instances.

In the following table is given a list of those towns or cities in which there is mention of a βουλή, the number of the inscription, and the date of each so far as they are known. It will be seen that these cities extend to every part of Macedonia, and, in point of time, the βουλή is met with, as a civil or governmental body in these cities during a period of at least six centuries.

Name of City	No. of Inscription	Date
Thasos	1130	Preceding the time of Alexander the Great
	1140, 1141	?
	1369	411 B.C.
Delos	671	220–215 B.C.
Lete	675	117 B.C.
Tzepikobon	258	97 A.D.
Thessalonica	365	143 A.D.
Edessa	1	182 A.D.
	37	?
Beroea	50, 51, 52	During the Roman period
Olynthus	744	?

As to the functions of the βουλή, members of it were frequently chosen as envoys. At Lete the βουλή prepared the προβούλευμα, but the politarchs presented it to the δῆμος (675:2-3). In Edessa the young men were formally registered as ἔφηβοι by a decree of the βουλή (1:1-6). In Tzepikobon the βουλή was convened by the politarchs (258). It had authority to receive legacies bequeathed to it for the benefit of the city. The βουλή had an officer who acted as treasurer for it (258). Upon the βουλή, sometimes in conjunction with the δῆμος, rested the responsibility of erecting public statues, setting up inscriptions, and in general, the care of public documents. They themselves did not personally take charge of the writing and setting up of inscriptions, or of the care of public documents, but they directed the officers who did take charge of all such work.

Thus far we have been considering the functions of the βουλή, but more often the βουλή and the δῆμος are represented as acting together. That the βουλή had functions distinct from those of the δῆμος is seen in the matter of their bringing forward a προβούλευμα for the consideration of the δῆμος (675:2-3), but for the most part they are mentioned as acting together. They seem always to have been associated with some city, but whether or not their jurisdiction extended beyond their own local city is not known. They seemed to constitute the final authority in all civil and political matters.

Two distinct usages of βουλή have been observed in the inscriptions. The one in which βουλή denotes counsel or plan occurs only in three inscriptions (37:8; 668:5; 1140:3) of a religious character. One of these (1140:3) is a modern Greek inscription, hence there are only two instances of this usage which pertain to the New Testament period. This usage finds a parallel in the common use of the term in the New Testament. Not only is the meaning of the word the same in both, but there is also this in common, that the literature in which they occur is in both cases religious; in one of the inscriptions (37) it is pretty certainly Christian religious ideas that find expression; in the other (668) a Greek religious atmosphere forms the background in which the usage occurs. The difference in the proportion of usages between the inscriptions and the New Testament is to be accounted for by the difference of their subject-matter.

The other usage is the one almost invariably found in the inscriptions, that is, with a technical meaning denoting a political body. The inscriptions are for the most part of an official character. They contain records which are of interest to the public, and which are generally given in a legal formula, and so the prevailing usage of βουλή is, in them, technical.

To this technical Macedonian usage there is a parallel, partial at least, in Palestinian usage where the chief governing body of the Jews was called a βουλή (Josephus, *B. J.*, II, xv, 6; II, xvi, 2; V, xiii, 1). Before reaching a final conclusion as to how far this parallel usage of the term βουλή denotes political bodies of like character and functions, it is necessary to examine the term βουλευτής, and also the terms γερουσία and συνέδριον, names by which the governing body of Jerusalem was designated.

I. B.   βουλευτής

The word βουλευτής occurs four times in the Macedonian inscriptions (671:77; 675:3, 49; 744:1).

(1)   671
        καὶ δοῦναι τὸν ἐπὶ τοὺς ἀγῶν[α]ς τῆι
75   μὲν ἀναγραφῆι τοῦ στεφάνου καὶ παρὰ . . . . των ισ(?)
        τηρων τῆι ἀναθέσει τῆς εἰκόνος ὃν ἂν [τόπον] δό[ξηι]
        τοῖς βουλευταῖς . . . . . .

The most of this inscription is preserved. The part here transcribed is sufficient to illustrate the usage of βουλευτής. For the place and date of the inscription, and for the translation and explanation of it see I. A. (9).

It is seen, from the passage quoted, that the place for the setting-up of the image was to be chosen by the βουλευταί. Of the precise significance of the term βουλευτής this passage affords us no clear indication, but it is doubtless safe to assume that here as elsewhere the term is an official designation denoting a member of the βουλή. The members of the βουλή of Athens were referred to by the term βουλευταί (Arist. Pol. 45. 3). Much additional evidence might be cited to show that, in Athens, βουλευτής was the term commonly used to designate a member of the βουλή. In the Macedonian inscriptions there are two instances which tend strongly to show that a similar usage of the term obtained in Macedonia. In 675:2–3 it is stated that the βουλευταί drew up the προβούλευμα. In Athens this was a matter which pertained distinctly to the functions of the βουλή. There seems then to be a high degree of probability that the βουλευταί here mentioned were the members of the βουλή of Lete.

In 744:1 reference is made to the fact that a man was twice a βουλευτής. It is well known that in Athens a man was eligible for membership in the βουλή only twice (Arist. 62. 3). The evident intention in the inscription cited was to show that Βαίβιος had received the honor of being appointed a βουλευτής as often as it was permitted any man to receive that honor. The usage of the term βουλευτής in Macedonia seems then to accord with that of Athens. In both places it was used to denote a member of the βουλή.

243]   27

(2)   675

2   Ληταίων οἱ πολιτάρχαι, προβουλευσαμέ-
         νων τῶν βουλευτῶν, εἶπαν.

                . . . .

49   καὶ εἰρέθησαν πρεσβευταὶ τῶν βουλευτῶν
         Ἄδαιος Ἀδαίου, Λύσων Φιλώτου, Ἀμύντας Λιέους.

The whole of this inscription is extant, but only the two clauses
containing the term βουλευτής are here transcribed. For the place
to which it belongs and its date see I.A. (10).

In the first reference, quoted above, it is stated that "the βουλευταί
having drawn up the προβούλευμα, the politarchs of Lete made the
motion." That is, the politarchs introduced, by a formal resolution,
the προβούλευμα at a meeting of the ἐκκλησία. In the latter clause,
"the envoys were chosen from the βουλευταί." These envoys were
delegated to convey to the Roman treasurer the vote of honor conferred
upon him by the βουλή and the δῆμος of Lete. In the discussion of
the preceding inscription it was seen that a βουλευτής was a member
of the βουλή. Here it appears that the βουλή or its members, the
βουλευταί drew up the προβούλευμα and that they were chosen as
envoys for the city.

(3)   744
                A. Baíβιος, βουλευτὴς δίς.

The whole of this inscription, consisting of five lines, is extant.
The first line is here transcribed. It was found at Olynthus in Macedonia.
The date is not known.

The man whose name appears in this inscription erected a monument
to the memory of his wife. As already pointed out the important
contribution which it makes is in showing that in Macedonia a man
might twice be elected a βουλευτής, and, by inference from this fact,
that it designates a member of the βουλή.

It thus appears that, generically, the term has the same meaning
in the inscriptions as in the New Testament, but that the specific
meaning is different. In both cases it is an official designation denoting
a member of a body having governmental functions. But whereas
in the inscriptions this body is the βουλή of a Greek city, in the New
Testament it is the highest legislative and judicial body of the Jewish
people, commonly called the Sanhedrin. It may perhaps be regarded
as most probable that the employment of βουλή in Josephus, and of

βουλευτής in Mark 15:43 for the Jewish Council and one of its members respectively, is not the reflection of a common usage in Jewish Greek terminology, but a transfer to a Jewish body and one of its members of a Greek term which in strict Greek usage had a similar, though not identical significance, somewhat as if we today should speak of one of the πολιτάρχαι of Thessalonica as the mayor of the city.   And Josephus may very well in this case be adapting his terminology to the common vocabulary of his readers.

II. γερουσία

The term γερουσια occurs twice in the Macedonian inscriptions
(1410:7; 1411:1).

(1)   1410

Ἀγαθῇ τύχῃ
τὴν ἀξιολογωτά-
την ἀρχιέρειαν
Μεμμίαν Βελληί-

5

ναυμ Ἀλεξάνδραν τὸ
σεμνότατον συν-
έδριον τῆς γερου-
σίας τὴν μητέρα
εὐτευχῶς.

The whole of this inscription is extant and is here transcribed. It
reads as follows: "With good luck, the most august συνέδριον erected
this monument in honor of the most noteworthy high priestess Memmia
Belleina Alexandra, the mother of the γερουσία, farewell."

In 1883 Mr. and Mrs. J. Theodore Bent discovered in Thasos a
triumphal arch in front of which there stood two pedestals. On the
southern base, on which a statue of more than life-size was placed, this
inscription was found. As to its date Dimitsas says: "ἀνήκει εἰς τὸν
β' . . . . γ' αἰῶνα μ. Χ." (Μακ., II, 965, n. 1410). E. L. Hicks
dates it within 212–17 A.D. (Jour. Hell. Studies, VIII, 1887, 424).

There is nothing given here to indicate that the γερουσία was
different, as respects its functions, from the βουλή of the other inscriptions. The earlier inscriptions found in Thasos designated the governmental body by the term βουλή, even when that council was an oligarchy
similar to the γερουσία of Sparta. Apparently the γερουσία here
referred to is the same body that at an earlier period was called βουλή,
the two names being interchangeable at this time.

(2)   1411

2   Ἡ γερουσία

The whole of this mortuary inscription is extant, containing twelve
lines, in the second of which the term γερουσία occurs. It belongs to

the same time and place as the preceding inscription. The translation is as follows: "With good luck. The γερουσία erected this monument to Flavia Vibia Sabina the most noteworthy chief priestess and from her ancestors incomparable, mother of the γερουσία, the first and only one of those who from all time shared in equal honors with the members of the γερουσία."

Here again the γερουσία is exercising the functions which were generally attributed to the βουλή, or to the βουλή and the δῆμος.

In Sparta the γερουσία was a council of twenty-eight members, besides the two kings (Hdt. 6. 57; Plut. Lyc. 5). Membership in it was limited to a certain class, that is to persons possessing a good social and financial standing, and the age required for admission to it was at least sixty years (Plut. Lyc. 26). Candidates for admission to it must be καλοὶ κἀγαθοί (Arist. Pol. 2. 9, 22, 46, Newman's ed.). Membership was for life. The body was not accountable to any superior authority, or to the people for its official acts (Arist. Pol. 2. 9; Plut. Lyc. 26; Polyb. 6. 45. 2). In the middle of the fourth century B.C. Demosthenes, in writing concerning the γερουσία of Sparta, pointed out that certain qualifications were necessary for membership in it; membership in it was bestowed as a prize, or reward of merit and that within the γερουσία itself all the members shared equal privileges. Müller compares the Council of the Areopagos to the γερουσία of Sparta—"Daher die Sittenaufsicht der alten Gerichte, wie des Areopagos in Athen, so der Gerusia zu Sparta" (Müller, Dorier, II, xi, 215). He also adds: "Die Gerusia richtete alle peinlichen Klagen, wie auch die meisten, die den Lebenswandel der Bürger betrafen." A list of members of the γερουσία is given by Le Bas in his Voyage en Grèce et en Asie Mineure, p. 173a.

The γερουσία had authority to pass sentence of death, and to it as a court of justice all cases of murder were brought. Aristotle in referring to the cases which come before the ephors for judgment says, οἱ δὲ γέροντες τὰς φονικάς (Arist. Pol. 3. 1. 10). There is evidence for the existence of a γερουσία at Ephesus, Crete, Elis, and Cnidus.

Sometimes the terms βουλή and γερουσία occur in the same inscription in such a way that it is difficult to decide whether both refer to the same body, or whether they point to the existence of a βουλή and a γερουσία side by side. Owing to the occurrence of both words CIG, 1241 Boeckh concludes (CIG, I, p. 610) that they denote different bodies, while Foucart regards the two as identical. In general, however, the terms βουλή and γερουσία are used with reference to different cities, and denote political bodies differing as to their organization and possessing somewhat different functions.

During the Greek period the governing body at Jerusalem was called a γερουσία. In a letter written by Antiochus the Great to Ptolemy in 200 B.C. the following reference to the γερουσία occurs: καὶ μετὰ τῆς γερουσίας ἀπαντησάντων (Jos., Ant., XII, iii, 3)—"Since the Jews, on our first entrance into their country, showed their friendship toward us; and when we came to their city received us in a splendid manner and came to meet us with their γερουσία." Antiochus V, in a letter to the Jews in 164 B.C., sends greetings to the γερουσία τῶν Ἰουδαίων (II Macc. 11:27): "King Antiochus to the γερουσία of the Jews and to the other Jews, greeting."

The following quotations will illustrate the position of prominence held by the γερουσία and in part the functions which it exercised: II Macc. 1:10: καὶ οἱ ἐν τῇ Ἰουδαίᾳ καὶ ἡ γερουσία καὶ Ἰούδας Ἀριστοβούλῳ —"And they who are in Judea, and the γερουσία and Judas, to Aristobulus."

II Macc. 4:44: οἱ πεμφθέντες τρεῖς ἄνδρες ὑπὸ τῆς γερουσίας—"the three men who were sent by the γερουσία."

I Macc. 12:6: Ἰωναθὰν ἀρχιερεὺς τοῦ ἔθνους καὶ ἡ γερουσία—"Jonathan the high priest of the nation, and the γερουσία, and the priests and the rest of the people of the Jews, unto their brethren the Spartans, greeting."

Judith 4:8: καὶ ἡ γερουσία παντὸς δήμου Ἰσραήλ—"And the children of Israel did as Joakim the high priest had commanded them and the γερουσία of all the people of Israel, who dwelt at Jerusalem."

Judith 11:14: τὴν ἄφεσιν παρὰ τῆς γερουσίας—"And they have sent some to Jerusalem, because they also that dwell there have done this thing, to bring to them the discharge from the γερουσία."

Judith 15:8: καὶ ἡ γερουσία τῶν υἱῶν Ἰσραήλ—"And Joakim the high priest, and the γερουσία of the children of Israel who dwelt at Jerusalem came to behold the good things which the Lord had showed to Israel."

As early as Antiochus the Great the council at Jerusalem was known as the γερουσία, and took an active part in all political, and religious matters of public interest. From 200 B.C., and possibly earlier, Greek writers were accustomed to speak of this Jewish Council as the γερουσία. The earliest definite reference to it is that of Antiochus in 200 B.C. It is quite probable that this body at Jerusalem owed its organization to the spread of Greek political ideas, and that the name γερουσία was first applied to it by the Greeks, but on both of these points there is a lack of trustworthy evidence. At all events, the name γερουσία was not peculiar to the Jewish people. The Spartans and other Doric states had from very early times been familiar with a γερουσία.

In the Septuagint the word γερουσία has been used twenty-five times as a translation for זְקֵנִי, and once for בְּנֵי, but this does not imply that there was any such organization of the elders in the Old Testament period as we find in the second century B.C.

In 200 B.C. when Antiochus the Great addressed a letter to the γερουσία at Jerusalem the terms βουλή and γερουσία were both familiar to Greek writers. The βουλή of Athens and the γερουσία of Sparta were two well-known political bodies, each having marked characteristics of its own. The term of office in the βουλή of Athens was one year, and its members were subject to examination for their official conduct. In the γερουσία of Sparta membership was for life, and was independent of any other authority.

The βουλή of Athens was composed of five hundred members and a man was eligible for membership in it at thirty years of age (Xen. *Mem.* I. 2. 35). As to the γερουσία of Sparta, a man must be at least sixty years old before he was admitted to it, and the number of its members was limited to twenty-eight. In other cities the number varied, but it was always small. It appears then that the βουλή was the more democratic organization, and the γερουσία the more aristocratic and exclusive.

That the governmental body at Jerusalem was, at this early date, called a γερουσία seems to indicate that it was more closely related, in its organization and functions, to the Doric γερουσία than to the βουλή of Athens. The historical development of the Council at Jerusalem tends to confirm this view.

About the middle of the first century B.C. a change seems to have occurred in the name of this council. In 57–55 B.C. Gabinius divided the whole of the Jewish ἔθνος into five σύνοδοι (*B. J.*, I, viii, 5), one of which was at Jerusalem. What Gabinius really did at this time is more clearly stated in *Ant.*, XIV, v, 4, where it is said that he divided τὸ ἔθνος into equal parts or divisions and appointed five συνέδρια, one of which was to be in Jerusalem. The term συνέδριον is here applied by Josephus to the council at Jerusalem, as well as to the other four. This is the language in which Josephus describes what Gabinius did, but it is not thereby necessarily the terminology of Gabinius himself. We cannot therefore affirm that the council at Jerusalem was designated as a συνέδριον by Gabinius.

In 47 B.C. Hyrcanus II was reappointed ἐθνάρχης of the Jews at Jerusalem. In that year he summoned Herod from Galilee to appear before the συνέδριον at Jerusalem to answer an accusation of murder which had been made against him (Jos., *Ant.*, XIV, ix, 3–5). Here, for the first time, so far as can be learned, the term συνέδριον is unmistakably used to designate the council at Jerusalem, formerly known as the γερουσία, for it is uncertain whether Gabinius himself used the term at the earlier date.

Elsewhere συνέδριον is frequently used to denote courts of justice. Hesychius defines συνέδριον by δικαστήριον. In Prov. 22:10, συνέδριον is used to translate דִּין. In the Mishna, Sanhedrin I. 5, סנהדריות לשבטים לשבטים = "courts for the tribes." The employment of συνέδριον to denote this council at Jerusalem may tend to show that there was a growing emphasis placed upon the judicial functions of the Council. In this connection it is important to observe that Le Bas et Waddington (*Inscr.* III, n. 1221) mention the βουλευταί and the συνεδροί as two distinct classes of officers. While, from the beginning of the first century B.C. συνέδριον seems to be the usual name for the Council at Jerusalem, yet it is not the only name by which it was designated. It was also called the γερουσία and the βουλή.

The term γερουσία occurs only once in the New Testament (Acts 5:21), and there has been much difference of opinion as to its meaning in that passage. The difficulty there arises from the fact that both συνέδριον and γερουσία are used, connected by καί. Either one of these words, if occurring by itself, would be readily understood as referring to the Sanhedrin. As it is, however, commentators are unable to agree as to its meaning here. Some of the passages already quoted under γερουσία may afford some light on its meaning in Acts, which reads: τὸ συνέδριον καὶ πᾶσαν τὴν γερουσίαν τῶν υἱῶν Ἰσραήλ. A phrase similar to the latter half of this occurs in Judith 15: 8, ἡ γερουσία τῶν υἱῶν Ἰσραήλ where it is evidently used as a designation for the Sanhedrin. A somewhat similar phrase, referring to the Sanhedrin is found in II Macc. 11:27, τῇ γερουσίᾳ τῶν Ἰουδαίων. These phrases show that so far as the form of expression in Acts is concerned, γερουσίαν τῶν υἱῶν Ἰσραήλ may denote the Sanhedrin. Meyer, Stier, Alford and others regard γερουσία, in Acts, as a more general term than συνέδριον, and include under it elders who were not members of the Sanhedrin. Lumby, in the "Cambridge Bible" series, takes συνέδριον as referring to another and smaller council than the Sanhedrin. Wendt takes both words as denoting the same council, with the καί as an explicative. Schürer thinks that both words certainly refer to the same body, and that either καί is to be taken as an explicative, or that the author of the Acts was mistaken in supposing that συνέδριον was a less comprehensive term than γερουσία. He inclines to accept the latter view.

Inasmuch as it has been shown that συνέδριον was, at this time, the name commonly used to designate the Sanhedrin, and that γερουσία, in almost the same phraseology as that used in the New Testament, was used to denote the Sanhedrin, there seems to be a high degree of probability in favor of the view that both terms denote the Sanhedrin in Acts. In addition to the above statement regarding the γερουσία it is seen in the inscriptions (1410:7; 1411:2) that it was used to denote the governmental body of a city as late as the beginning of the third century A.D.

As respects the term συνέδριον it is found only once in the inscriptions (1410:6). For place and date and translation of this inscription see II. (1). It may there have one of two possible meanings. Either it was used to denote assembly in the general sense of that term, or it was used in the technical sense denoting the governmental body of the city. The former alternative, taking it in the more general sense, is apparently the correct interpretation.

In the first mention which we have of συνέδριον as a name for the Council at Jerusalem it is with reference to its exercising the functions of a court of justice, and in later times it is used with increasing frequency to designate a court of justice. In the New Testament it occurs twenty-two times, and, in all but three instances, it is used of the Council at Jerusalem in its exercise of judicial functions. Twice it is used of the local courts (Matt. 10:17; Mark 13:9), and once it occurs with the meaning of a session or a meeting of the Sanhedrin (John 11:47).

Notwithstanding this almost uniform usage of the New Testament it is seen that Josephus uses all three terms, βουλή, γερουσία, and συνέδριον to denote the Sanhedrin. Under the term βουλή he refers to it in (1) B. J., II, xv. 6: καὶ μεταπεμψάμενος τούς τε ἀρχιερεῖς καὶ τὴν βουλήν. Here, Florus, the Roman procurator at Jerusalem, sent for the priests and the βουλή to arrange terms of peace. (2) B. J., II, xvi. 2: ἔνθα καὶ Ἰουδαίων οἵ τε ἀρχιερεῖς ἅμα τοῖς δυνατοῖς καὶ ἡ βουλὴ παρῆν δεξιουμένη τὸν βασιλέα. On this occasion the chief priests, together with the men of power, and the βουλή came to meet King Agrippa and Neopolitanus, a Roman envoy, to present to them their grievances against Florus. (3) In *B. J.*, II, xiv. 1, the local courts are referred to under the term βουλή. In *B. J.*, II, xvii. 1, the term βουλευταί is used with reference to the Sanhedrin. (4) In *B. J.*, V, xiii, 1, the γραμματεύς of the βουλή was put to death by Simon during the war with Rome. This has an additional interest for us in the fact that it shows the existence of the office of γραμματεύς of the βουλή in Jerusalem.

The term γερουσία occurs, at least, three times in Josephus: *Ant.*, IV, viii. 16: αἱ ἀρχαὶ τῶν πόλεων . . . . , καὶ ἡ γερουσία . . . . οἱ ἱερεῖς καὶ οἱ Λευῖται καὶ ἡ γερουσία τῆς πόλεως ἐκείνης. This passage states that if a murder had been committed, and the murderer could not be found, that the ἀρχαί and the γερουσία of the nearest adjoining cities or towns were required to measure the distance, from where the murdered man was found, to these cities, and the one nearest to where the murdered man lay was then required to perform the following rite: The ἱερεῖς, the Λευῖται and the γερουσία were to wash their hands over the head of a slain heifer, and publicly proclaim themselves innocent of the blood of the dead man. From this it appears that each city had a γερουσία, and that the γερουσία in these cities had to deal with judicial matters, and with religious rites. In this instance the γερουσία is represented as co-operating with other officers in trying to determine who was responsible for the murder, but it is not, strictly speaking, acting in a judicial capacity. In *Ant.* XII, iii, 3, Antiochus is calling attention to the good-will shown to him by the Jews, who with their γερουσία came out to meet him. The paragraph in *Ant.*, XIII, v. 8 is of special interest to us in this discussion inasmuch as the βουλή of Rome, the γερουσία of Jerusalem, and the γερουσία of Sparta are all mentioned. Two envoys (πρεσβευταί), members of the γερουσία of Jerusalem, were sent to Rome in 144 B.C. to renew a treaty made under Onias I, and they were to go on a similar errand to Sparta. At Rome these envoys were received by the βουλή, and at Sparta by the γερουσία. All three of these bodies, the βουλή of Rome, the γερουσία of Sparta and the γερουσία of Jerusalem are represented as acting in a political capacity, each having authority to arrange treaties for their respective cities. The sending of this embassy took place about a century before there is any explicit mention of a συνέδριον at Jerusalem, or more accurately, before the Council at Jerusalem is called by that name. At that time γερουσία was the common name for the Council at Jerusalem, and Josephus in describing the event may be using the terms which were used in 144 B.C.

Josephus also refers to the Sanhedrin under the term συνέδριον: *Ant.*, XIV, ix. 3–5, εἰ μὴ πρότερον κατακριθείη τοῦτο παθεῖν ὑπὸ τοῦ συνεδρίου. The authority to pass the sentence of death is here ascribed to the συνέδριον of Jerusalem. In the two paragraphs following this one the word συνέδριον occurs eight times denoting the Sanhedrin of Jerusalem, and once the plural is used with reference to the members of the Sanhedrin. In *Ant.*, XV, vi, 2, it is implied that the συνέδριον at Jerusalem had authority to pass sentence of death upon a criminal. In *Ant.*, XX, ix, i, the word συνέδριον occurs twice, with reference to its passing sentence of death upon James the Just. But it appears that this sentence could not be executed without the consent of the Roman procurator, Albinus, and it happened on this occasion that Albinus revoked the sentence of death passed by the συνέδριον of Jerusalem.

In Josephus, as well as in the New Testament, the term συνέδριον denotes the Sanhedrin acting in a judicial capacity, and never as a legislative or civic body. This coincidence is all the more remarkable inasmuch as Josephus uses other terms, βουλή and γερουσία to denote the Sanhedrin exercising political or governmental functions. This investigation tends to show that the term συνέδριον as it was employed in the New Testament period to designate the council at Jerusalem, was used with reference to it as a judicial body, and that when this council was referred to as exercising civic or governmental functions it was commonly called the βουλή or the γερουσία. It seems to be highly probable that from about the middle of the first century B.C. the name συνέδριον became the common designation for the council at Jerusalem, but the earlier name, γερουσία, still survived side by side with the new, with perhaps a more distinct reference to its legislative functions.

III. δῆμος

The word δῆμος is found in sixteen of the Macedonian inscriptions, and in these it occurs thirty-seven times, or including five restorations by the editor, forty-two times. The following table gives a list of the inscriptions containing δῆμος, the name of the city to which each belongs, and their respective dates. In some instances the dates are given only approximately, as the exact date cannot always be ascertained. Further investigation may also change some of the dates which are here accepted.

No. of Inscription	Name of City	Date of Inscription
50........	Beroea	
52........	"	
365........	Thessalonica	143 A.D.
371........	Delos	220–215 B.C.
672........	"	" " "
675........	Aïvati	117 B.C.
847........	Amphipolis	358–357 B.C.
927........	"	Probably the early part of the Roman era
1080........	Ocra	Uncertain, probably before the Roman period
1085........	"	" " " " "
1130........	Thasos	Before the time of Alexander the Great
1338........	"	Between 42 B.C. and 27 B.C.
1339........	"	First century A.D.
1340........	"	" " "
1369........	"	411 B.C.

It thus appears that five of the cities of Macedonia had a δῆμος, or seven if we, with Dimitsas, include Delos and Thasos. As to the period of time covered by these inscriptions they extend from the last part of the fifth century B.C. to the first half of the second century A.D., and perhaps later.

In the treatment of the word βουλή, the relation of the βουλή to the δῆμος was discussed. It there appeared that the βουλή had certain functions pertaining to it as a distinct body, but that more often the βουλή and the δῆμος were represented as acting together in the transaction of public matters. On other occasions official action is attributed to the δῆμος alone. The functions of the δῆμος in so far as they appear in these inscriptions are as follows:

1. The δῆμος was the highest political authority in city or state. In 255:10–14 the action of the βουλή on this occasion seems to have had the force of a motion or a proposition, according to modern terminology. It was introduced at a meeting of the δῆμος in the form of a resolution, and carried with it the recommendation of the βουλή, but it did not become an authoritative decree until the δῆμος had voted upon it.

2. The δῆμος had authority to pass decrees honoring benefactors of the city (671:12–19).

3. At Thessalonica the δῆμος chose the place where the statue was to be erected (671:38–41).

4. The δῆμος at Thasos (in 411 B.C.) had authority to grant exemption from taxation (1369:1–2), and to punish by exile (1369:5). These decrees of the δῆμος were repealed by the oligarchy in 411 B.C., but the supremacy of this revolutionary body was of short duration. Reference is here made to the δῆμος which was in Thasos before the oligarchy was established, and not to the δῆμος appointed by the oligarchical βουλή.

5. The δῆμος at Amphipolis and Ocra erected monuments in honor of their benefactors, at their own expense (927:4; 1080:2; 1085:1).

6. The δῆμος of Thasos exercised both judicial and legislative functions (1369).

The only suggestion as to how the δῆμος was appointed is to be found in Thasos (1369), where it appears that the βουλή was to make out a list of those who should be permitted to take the oath as members of the δῆμος. Inasmuch as this took place during the revolution of the oligarchy it cannot be assumed that this was the regular order of procedure. It is seen, however, that the δῆμος is always associated with some city of which it is the highest governing body, and with respect to the βουλή they sustained the same relation to each other in matters of government as the βουλή and the δῆμος of Athens did to each other. In Athens it is a well-known fact that the δῆμος included practically all the citizens of the place. Every adult Athenian was entitled to attend, and formed part of the body, as in a New England town meeting (cf. Gilbert, Greek Const. Ant., pp. 285–90). The δῆμος of the Macedonian cities was in all probability made up in this way. The citizens thus legislated for themselves, and were not a representative body.

From the usage of the term δῆμος in the inscriptions certain facts are obtained which have a bearing upon the meaning and usage of

this term in the New Testament. It occurs four times in the New
Testament (Acts 12:22; 17:5; 19:30, 33). In Acts 12:22 it pertains
to the city of Caesarea in Palestine; in 17:5 to Thessalonica in Macedonia; and in 19:30, 33 to Ephesus in Asia Minor. The Macedonian
inscriptions show that the cities of Macedonia were generally governed
by a body called ὁ δῆμος. Reference is made in No. 365 to the δῆμος
of Thessalonica. Ephesus not being a Macedonian city is not mentioned
here, but there are other inscriptions which make mention of a βουλή
and a δῆμος in Ephesus. Not only do the inscriptions show that a
political body called the δῆμος existed in Thessalonica and Ephesus,
but they also afford some light as to some of the officers mentioned in
the New Testament.

The politarchs are associated with the high priest in such a way as to
suggest that they were colleagues, but that the high priest was in some
manner their superior officer. The statement is made (365) that certain
things were done for the βουλή and the δῆμος by the politarchs περὶ τὸν
ἀρχιερέα. Both the politarchs and the high priest were subordinate,
or subject to the authority of the δῆμος. They were both officers of
the city.

The accusation against Paul and Silas in Thessalonica was political.
They had violated certain civic laws and so were answerable to the city
for their conduct. The intention seems to have been to bring them to
the δῆμος for judgment, but failing to find Paul and Silas, they arrested
Jason, together with some of the brethren, for having given shelter to
Paul and Silas. Jason was brought to the politarchs for trial. Evidently it was to the politarchs as public officers under the δῆμος that
Jason was summoned. They were judicial officers of the δῆμος, that
is of the δῆμος as a political body. There seems to be a strong probability that the term δῆμος in Acts 17:5 has its technical meaning denoting
a governmental body.

In favor of the technical meaning in Acts 19:30, 33 it is seen from
the inscriptions: (1) that one of the regular places of meeting for the
δῆμος was the theater (with Acts 19:29 cf. CIA, II, 378, 381, 392,
403, 408, 435, 439, 454, 468, 471); (2) that all matters of interest to
the city were to be disposed of, either at a regular session of the δῆμος
or at a meeting specially called, in case of emergency (cf. Gilbert,
Greek Const. Ant., pp. 285–87); therefore the purpose for which the
δῆμος is assembled on any occasion was legislative or judicial; (3) the
usual name for an assembly of the δῆμος was ἐκκλησία (198, 255, 671).
The meeting of the δῆμος in Ephesus is designated as an ἐκκλησία,

but by implication an unlawful ἐκκλησία (Acts 19:32, 39, 41).   In this case we must understand that it was an irregular meeting of the δῆμος, not convened in any regular order.

Most of the reasons given for interpreting δῆμος in a technical sense in Acts, chaps. 17 and 19 would apply to its usage in Acts 12:22.   The data furnished by the inscriptions tend to confirm the interpretation of δῆμος in Acts as a technical term denoting a political body.

IV.   διαθήκη¹

(1)   128
                 Ἡρακλίδης Ἀσκληπιά-
                 δου ἱερεὺς τῆς θεοῦ
                 κατὰ δι[α]θή[κη]ν ἐκ-
                 έλευσεν.

The whole of this inscription is extant and is here transcribed. It was found in Janitza (Πέλλη). The date is not known, but there is nothing in the inscription itself to suggest a late date. The priest of the goddess provided κατὰ διαθήκην for something to be done. In many of the Macedonian monumental inscriptions the object of the verb is omitted when that object is the tomb or monument on which the inscription is written. It is more frequently omitted than mentioned in such cases. In the above inscription the object of the verb if stated would be some word or words concerning the erection of the monument. There is no express mention here of the disposition of property, though the natural inference is that when the testator commanded that certain things should be done that he provided the money necessary for doing it.

(2)   258
κ(αὶ) Φίλωνος τοῦ Κόνωνος ποιησαμένου λόγους περ(ὶ) Μ. Οὐετίου Φίλωνος τοῦ θείου κ(αὶ) προσανγείλαντος ὅτι κ(αὶ) πρώ(ην) τὴν ἑαυτοῦ πατρ(ίδα)
ἐτείμησε μεγάλως κ(αὶ) τελευτῶν οὐδὲ τῆς κατὰ τὴν βουλὴν τε(ι)μῆς ἠμέλησεν, ἀλλ᾽ ἀφῆκεν αὐτῇ κατὰ διαθήκην Δ´: αφ: ἐφ᾽ ᾧ ἐκ τῶν κατ᾽ ἐνιαυτὸν
ἐξ αὐτῶν γεινομένων τόκων ἡμέραν ἄγουσα Οὐεττίου Βωλανοῦ ἑορτάσιμον εὐ-
ωχῆται τῇ πρὸ δεκατεσσάρων καλανδῶν Νοεμβρίων, ἔδοξεν τῇ βουλῇ τὴν τοῦ
ἀνδρὸς σεμνότητα κ(αὶ) βούλησιν ἀποδέξασθαι ἐπί τε ταῖς ὑπ᾽ αὐτοῦ κατὰ τὴν
διαθήκην γεγραμμέναις αἱρέσεσιν τὸ τάργύριον λαβεῖν καὶ κατ᾽ ἐνιαυτὸν ἄγειν
τὴν τοῦ Οὐεττίου Βωλανοῦ ἑορτάσιμον ἐκ τῶν τόκων ἡμέραν καὶ μήτε τοῦ
προγεγραμμένου κεφαλαίου ἀπαναλίσκειν τι εἰς ἑτέραν χρείαν μήτε τοῦ κατ᾽
ἐνιαυτὸν γινομένου τόκου, ἀλλ᾽ ὡς ὁ δοὺς Φίλων ἠθέλησεν, τὸ τάργύριον
ἠριθμήσατο καὶ παρέλαβεν ὁ ἐπιμελητὴς τῶν τῆς βουλῆς δηναρίων Λούκιος
Λουκρήτιος Πούδης.

¹ For a thorough discussion of the term διαθήκη see F. O. Norton, *Lexicographical and Historical Study of* διαθήκη.

The whole of this inscription is extant, and from l. 7 to the end is here transcribed. For the place and date of this inscription see I. (6), where a translation is also given of ll. 9–26.

A longer portion of this inscription is here transcribed because it is the best example of a διαθήκη found in the Macedonian inscriptions, and its importance is enhanced by the fact that it comes so near to the time when the books of the New Testament were written. From it we learn that a certain man when dying left to the βουλή, κατὰ διαθήκην, 1,500 denarii, on the condition that from the accruing interest an annual festival was to be conducted at a stated time. The βουλή voted to accept the money on the conditions named in the διαθήκη, and to use it only as directed by the testator. Express mention is made (l. 10) of the death of the testator, which is rather unusual, although it is always assumed that the διαθήκη becomes effective only on the death of the testator. It is seen that at this time a man could dispose of a part, at least, of his property to some person or persons apart from his heir. Property might be transmitted by means of a διαθήκη. This bequest to the βουλή was conditional, and could be used by the βουλή only by carrying out the conditions named in the διαθήκη. A similar transaction, so far as the city is concerned, takes place today when a city accepts a gift from Andrew Carnegie agreeing to fulfil the conditions attaching to the gift. The transaction between the βουλή and the testator was not mutual. The testator took the initiative, named the recipient or beneficiary, and the conditions attaching to it, and his terms were authoritative.

(3)   281
                              τὰ τέ-
κνα Τι(βέριος) Κλαύδιος Πρόκλος, Μάξιμ-
ος Κλαύδιος καὶ Αἰλία
6   Πρόκλα ἡ σύμβιος κατὰ διαθήκας,

Only a part of this inscription is extant, and only that portion of it is transcribed which contains the term διαθήκη. It was found in a church in Mpeloboditsa which lies between Prilapos and Stobos. The date is not known, but the Latin names indicate that it belongs to the Roman period.

It is said in the inscription that, "Tiberius Claudius Phortius, having done duty as a soldier in a praetorium, his children, Tiberius Claudius

Proclus, Maximus Claudius and Ailia Procla his wife erected [this monument,] κατὰ διαθήκας."

This is a monumental rather than a testamentary inscription. The purpose of the inscription is to record the fact that the children of the deceased had erected a monument to the memory of their father who had been a soldier, but they did this in accordance with the commands of their father as expressed in his διαθήκη. The matter of erecting a monument to the deceased does not seem, in this case, to have been left to the discretion of his heirs, but was made obligatory upon them, by the testator in his διαθήκη. The mention of the διαθήκη is then incidental to the main purpose of this inscription, and is not a statement regarding the διαθήκη as such.

The two sons and a son's wife are recorded as having erected the monument. They were in all probability his heirs, although nothing is said about the disposition of property. That would be aside from the purpose of the inscription. The plural number of διαθήκη, which occurs in l. 6, does not seem to differ in its meaning from the singular. The two forms seem to be used interchangeably. That there was at one time a difference between the singular number of διαθήκη and the plural number of it is altogether probable, but that difference is not apparent in any of these inscriptions.

(4)   348

'Ιούλιος (καὶ) Θηίγονος
Ποπλίῳ Φρον-
τίν- τῷ πατρώ-
ῳ κατὰ τὸν θ[εῖον] ὁρ-
5   κισμὸν τῆς διαθή-
κης τὸν βωμὸν
ἔκτισαν καὶ τὰ θεῖ-
α αὐτῷ ἐποίησαν.

The whole of this inscription is extant, and is transcribed. It was found in the house of Chrestos Sabba in Achrida, which lies to the north of the earlier town of Lychnidus, which was the chief town of the Dasaretae in Illyricum. The Roman names occurring in it indicate that it belongs to the Roman period. It reads as follows: "Julius and Theigonus for Poplius Frontinus their father built the altar and performed the sacred rites according to the divine adjuration of the διαθήκη."

The purpose of the inscription seems to be to record the fact that the sons have fulfilled their obligation to their deceased father, in accordance with the solemn injunction imposed upon them in the διαθήκη. These commands enjoined by the testator upon his heirs seem to have authority, and are in all probability conditions which they must fulfil before they can enter upon the inheritance, as in the case of the property left to the βουλή of Tzepikobon. They have the force of an authoritative command, and were not to be lightly disregarded by the son or heir. This inscription tends to show that the sons were expected and required to maintain the religious duties of the deceased parent, and that a man might make provision in his διαθήκη for the perpetuation of the obligations resting upon his family.

(5)   369
6   ἐκ διαθηκῶν Ἐρεννί[ου

Only a part of this inscription is extant, in a very fragmentary condition. For a description of it, and for its place and date see under I. (7) where an inscription referring to the same time and event is described, or, more accurately perhaps, they are both copies of the same original. See *Jour. Hell. Studies*, VIII, 1887, 362.

Although the details of this transaction cannot be obtained, yet it is reasonably certain that a bequest was made in favor of the city of Thessalonica, for the establishing of certain games. The preposition ἐκ occurs here before διαθηκῶν, instead of the more usual construction of κατά with the accusative, but apparently with little difference in meaning.

The word διαθήκη occurs in five of these inscriptions, in one of which it is found twice. These inscriptions in which διαθήκη occurs either relate to the duties of children to their deceased parents, or have reference to bequests made to some city, and so have a public interest. They were not intended to set forth the διαθήκη itself, or even to describe it as such. They afford, however, considerable indirect evidence as to the character of the διαθήκη.

There is only one explicit reference to the disposition of property (258), and in that case mention of the bequest is made subordinate to the purpose for which it was given. The main feature of the διαθήκη, as here presented, is that it gives to the children or legatees certain specific and binding commands which they are required to fulfil. It has been seen that the children were solemnly adjured in the διαθήκη to perform the sacred rites to their deceased father. I am uncertain whether this expression implies that these rites were observed by the sons as worship to their father, or whether it means that they performed the rites for their father, in his interest. In two instances it is the city which is placed under obligation to carry out the wishes of the testator. There seems to be a strong probability that these injunctions had in every case a religious significance, and had to do with the perpetuation of the family life. The most noticeable feature of the διαθήκη as it appears in the Macedonian inscriptions is that it always contains certain injunctions or commands which are to be executed after the decease of the person who gave them, and that these requirements are imposed without consulting the persons who are to execute them.

The discussion of the difficult question as to what sense or senses the word bears in the New Testament lies outside the scope of this paper. It must suffice to remark concerning the διαθήκη of these inscriptions:

1. That it is testamentary rather than contractual. It is not a mutual compact to which both parties give assent, mutually contracting to do certain things, but the act of one person giving charges to another, or bestowing property on another, or both of these. The initiative is always taken by the one person.

2. The thing enjoined in the διαθήκη is apparently always to be executed after the decease of the testator. His death is seldom explicitly mentioned, but is always assumed as the *terminus a quo* of the enjoined act.

3. When property is bequeathed it may be accompanied by a charge to be fulfilled, and in such a way that the commission must be accepted in order to obtain the property (258). It is not clear that these injunctions always have a relation to the obtaining of a bequest. The injunctions laid upon children of the testator seem to be imperative, but perhaps in all these cases some property is left to the sons.

4. The usage of the term διαθήκη in the inscriptions is similar to its usage in the Old and New Testaments in that the initiative is always taken by one person. In the scriptures it is God who takes the initiative, and in the inscriptions it is the testator. In both there is some disposition made. It is also similar in that, in both, certain duties are enjoined upon the children or heirs. The one making the διαθήκη always assumes the right to command, and to withhold his bequest if the conditions attached to it are not fulfilled.

V.   δόγμα

(1)   1

6   κατὰ τὸ δόγμα τῆς βουλῆς

For place and date, and translation of the inscription from which this phrase is transcribed see I. (1). According to this inscription an enrolment of the names of those who had become ἔφηβοι during a certain year was made by a δόγμα of the βουλή. The term δόγμα is here used in a technical sense, and denotes an official decree.

(2)   217

                 —μηδὲ δόγ-
μα τινὶ διδόνι πολιτείας ἢ χρήσε-
ως τῶν δημοσίων,

. . . .
            Ἐὰν δὲ τῇ . . . . .
40   . . . . . πολειτάρχῃ καὶ δόγμα . . . . .
       . . . . δημόσια,

. . . .
45   . . . . . . τοῦτο τὸ δόγμα ἔ-
δοξε τῷ διέποντι
τὴν ἐπαρ-
χίαν Ἰουνίῳ Ῥουφίνῳ διά

All of this inscription is extant except the last four lines, of which only a word or two remain, but the extant portion is badly mutilated. Only the immediate contexts in which the word δόγμα occurs are transcribed. It was found in Idranitzi, and belongs to Orestis, which lies about one hundred miles to the west of Thessalonica. Sakellarios who first published it assigns it to the reign of Hadrian (117–138 A.D.).

It is a decree passed by the πολῖται and the πολιτάρχης regarding the right of possession to certain lands, "concerning which those who hold them in possession formerly made a compact giving them up and handing them over to the state; but now the more powerful men of the eparchy are driving out by violence the poor, which is not lawful for them" (ll. 9–18). The decree provides that the land shall remain in the possession of the Orestae to whom it formerly belonged, and that

263]   47

"the politarch holding office for the year shall have charge of these
things, to cast out and to hinder those using violence" (ll. 34–39).
Beginning at the middle of l. 45 it reads: "this δόγμα was decreed by
Junius Rufinus who is filling the office of eparch."

This δόγμα is an authoritative protest on the part of the people
against certain acts of injustice which deprived them of their lands.
It discloses the fact that the citizens had a right to legislate for themselves; the government was not in the hands of an aristocracy. Ll. 39–
44 seem to provide against a decree which shall annul or in any way set
aside the decree passed by the politarch and the citizens.

(3)   258

3   δόγμ(α)τος ἀν(α)γραφῇ τῇ ιά τοῦ Δαισίου μηνός

The whole of this inscription is extant, and the phrase containing
the word δόγμα is transcribed. For place and date of this inscription,
and a translation of a portion of it see under I. (6).

The line transcribed above relates that the δόγμα was inscribed on
the eleventh of the month Daisios in the year 243. By this δόγμα of
the βουλή a bequest to the city was accepted. The term δόγμα is
here employed in its ordinary technical meaning, denoting an official
decree.

(4)   398

4   οὐκ ἔφυγον δὲ δόγμα τὸ . .
            τοῖσι μίτοις

The whole of this inscription is extant, but only the clause containing the term δόγμα is transcribed. It was found in the modern town of
Καλλί-Κουλέ, but where and when it was first written does not seem
to be known. It reads thus: "My parents called me Droson, always
rejoicing with gentle heart, but I knew a short light of life, and escaped
not the decree of the fates, and I passed seventeen years of life, but now
I lie in Hades sharing neither good nor evil."

Generically the term δόγμα seems to have the same usage here as
in the other inscriptions, but whereas in those it denotes the authoritative decree of a governmental body, it here denotes a decree of the fates,
which is absolute and binding.

The term δόγμα is found in four of the Macedonian inscriptions,
and occurs six times in all. Twice it is used of a decree of the βουλή
(1, 258); once of a decree by the πολῖται and the πολιτάρχης (217);

twice with reference to a decree by an individual acting in an official capacity (217:28-32; 39-41) and once it is used of a decree by the fates. The usage of the term δόγμα in the inscriptions is parallel to that of the New Testament, in which it occurs five times, four times in the plural number (Acts 16:4; 17:7; Eph. 2:15; Col. 2:14), and once in the singular (Luke 2:1). In Luke 2:1 and Acts 17:7 the δόγμα is issued by an individual, a ruler. In Acts 16:4 the decrees (δόγματα) are from the apostles and elders together with the whole church at Jerusalem. Their action on this occasion is regarded by the writer of the Acts as an authoritative utterance. A position of authority over other Christians was ascribed to the leaders and the church at Jerusalem. Specifically it is different from the authority attributed to the βουλή of a Greek city, but generically, the authority ascribed to the δόγμα is the same in both instances.

In Eph. 2:15 the statutes referred to are those found in the Mosaic law, which were currently regarded as coming from God through Moses, and as possessing divine authority. When reference is made to the decrees or statutes of the Mosaic code the plural denotes a group or body of statutes, but when the reference is to the decrees of the elders and apostles it denotes the several commands issued by them.

It appears then that underlying the usage of this term, both in the inscriptions and in the scriptures, there is the idea of an authoritative utterance. It is also a matter of interest to know that δόγμα was not used of decrees made by the Athenian ἐκκλησία. They were called ψηφίσματα.

VI.   δοκέω

                                 198
3   Ἔδοξεν τῇ βουλῇ καὶ τῷ δήμῳ
       . . . .
6   [ε]ἴτε φόρον δοκεῖ τάττειν τὸν δῆμον αὐτ-
       ίκ]α μάλα,
       . . . .
18   εἰπεῖν δὲ Περδίκκᾳ ὅτι δοκε[ῖ δίκα-
       ιον] εἶναι
       . . . .
32   Ἔδοξεν τῇ βουλῇ καὶ τῷ δήμ-
       ῳ]
       . . . .
48   ὅ τι[ἂν δο-
       κ]ῇ [ἄξι]ον εἶναι περὶ Μεθωναίων,
       . . . .
56   Ἔδο-
       ξεν τῇ] βουλῇ καὶ [τ]ῷ [δ]ήμ[ῳ]
       . . . .

                                 199
5   . . . . . . ἔδοξε τῇ βουλῇ καὶ τῷ
       δήμῳ . . . .

                                 217
24   ἔδοξε τῷ τε πολειτάρχῃ
       καὶ τοῖς πολείταις ὁμογνωμονοῦ-
       σι·
       . . . .
45   τοῦτο τὸ δόγμα ἔ-
       δοξε τῷ διέποντι τὴν ἐπαρ-
       χίαν Ἰουνίῳ Ῥουφίνῳ . . . . .

                                 255
4   Ἔδοξεν τῆι βουλῆι καὶ τῶι δήμωι,
       . . . .
12   ὅτι δοκεῖ τῆι βουλῆι ἐπαινέσαι με-
       [ν αὐ]τόν,

                    50   [266

258

16   . . . . . ἔδοξεν τῇ βουλῇ
τὴν τοῦ ἀνδρὸς σεμνότητα κ(αὶ) βούλησιν
ἀποδέξασθαι . . . .

. . . .

352

2   ἐκ τῆς δοκούσης
τάχα τιμίας ὕλης

. . . .

671

1   Ἔδοξεν τῆι βουλῆι καὶ τῶι δήμωι·

. . . .

6   δεδόχθαι
τῆι βουλῆι καὶ τῶι δήμωι·

. . . .

20   Ἔδοξεν τῆι βουλῆι καὶ δήμωι·

. . . .

27   δεδόχθαι τῆι βουλῆι
καὶ τῶι δήμωι

. . . .

δοῦναι τόπον ὡς
βέλτιστον καὶ τοῖς δεδογμένοις ἀκολούθως δια-
70   λεγέντος καὶ Βούλωνος· δεδόχθαι τῆι βουλεῖ·

. . . .

77   τῆι ἀναθέσει τῆς εἰκόνος ὃν ἂν [τόπον]
δό[ξηι] τοῖς βουλευταῖς.

675

36   Δι' ὃ δεδόχθαι Ληταίων τῆι βουλῆι καὶ τῶι δήμωι . . . .

742

22   . . . . . ἐὰν ἀμ]φοτέροις δοκῇ . . . . .

829

65   . . . . Δοκεῖ δέ μοι . . . . .

. . . .

69   τοῦτο ἐμοὶ δοκεῖ τῆς ἀγαθῆς τύχης ἔργον εἶναι.

77   Συμβέβηκέ τοίνυν τὰ δοκοῦντα τῆς
κώμης ταύτης πλεονεκτήματα

267

847
1   Ἔδοξεν τῷ δήμῳ

976
2   [Ἔ]δοχσεν τῆι β[ο]υ[λῆι] καὶ τôι δήμοι,

. . . .

53   ὅτι ἂν δοκεῖ ἀγαθ[ὸν ἄλλο ὅτι ἂν δέονται]

977
8   [Ἔδο]ξεν [τῇ] βουλῇ καὶ τῷ δήμῳ

. . . .

15   [ὅτι δοκει τῇ β]ουλῇ,

1130
5   δεδόχθἁι τῇ βουλῇ καὶ τῷ δήμῳ.

. . . .

13   τά τε δόξαντα ἄκυρα ἔστω

Inasmuch as the word δοκέω occurs, for the most part, in a constantly recurring formula it is not necessary for the understanding of its meaning or usage to quote a larger context in each case, or to give a description of each inscription in which it occurs. Under III. (2), where the context is transcribed, an illustration of its common usage in the technical sense may be found.

It occurs thirty-two times in the Macedonian inscriptions, and is generally used of the expression of opinion in the sense of a public or official decree. There are however two other distinct usages of the word in the inscriptions. These three usages are found as follows:

1. It is used with the technical meaning in referring to official acts in the following inscriptions: 198:3, 6, 18, 32, 48, 56; 199:5; 217:24, 45; 255:4, 12; 258:16; 671:1, 6, 20, 27, 69, 70, 77; 675:36; 742:22; 829:77; 847:1; 976:2; 977:8, 15; 1130:5, 13.

2. It is employed in impersonal expressions in which it does not have the technical meaning, as in 829:65, 69, δοκεῖ δέ μοι, and ἐμοὶ δοκεῖ where it is equivalent to "methinks," "it seems to me."

3. Twice it is used in referring to things with the meaning of "to be reputed" or "esteemed" (352:2; 976:53).

When the word is used as in No. 1 above it is intended to denote an act of authority which for governmental purposes has the force of a law. It expresses an opinion which is public and official and not private or personal. Such authoritative declarations are made by some body, or individual, having the right, by virtue of his office, to issue such decrees.

These official acts or decrees may come from: (1) the βουλή and the δῆμος (198:3, 6, 18, 48, 56); (2) the βουλή (255:12); (3) the δῆμος (847:1); (4) the πολιτάρχης and the πολῖται (217:24); (5) an individual ruler (217:45).

Of the three distinct usages in the inscriptions each has a parallel in the New Testament. Generically, the usage of δοκέω in Acts 15:22, 25, 28 is the same as that mentioned in No. 1 above. That an expression of so technical and legal a character should be used in the Acts passage is of interest in indicating the attitude of authority which the leaders of the church at Jerusalem assumed, or which the author of the Acts supposed them to take. Yet it would doubtless be overpressing this to make an exact equivalence between their authority and that of the βουλή of a Greek city. Nevertheless, it does indicate, in the view of the writer of the Acts, that the church at Jerusalem had assumed an attitude of authority over the gentile Christians outside of Jerusalem.

A usage parallel to No. 2 is found in Acts 25:27.

In Gal. 2:9; Mark 10:42 the word occurs with the meaning of "to be reputed" or "esteemed" as in No. 3 above.

It thus appears that of the usages found in the inscriptions all are paralleled in the New Testament, but that the proportion of usages is very different. A usage occurring but three times out of sixty-two instances in the New Testament appears in the inscriptions twenty-eight out of thirty-two occurrences of the word. What might seem from the New Testament to be an exceptional usage is shown by the inscriptions not to be so at all. The difference in frequency is the natural result of the difference in the character of the literature.

VII.   ἐκκλησία

(1)   671

50   καὶ παρελθόντος εἰς τὴν ἐκκλησίαν καὶ
          διαλεγέντος ἀκολούθως τοῖς ἐψηφισμένοις,

All of this inscription is extant. For a translation and description of it, and for its place and date see I. A. (9). On this occasion the envoy (πρεσβευτής) from Delos was received by the ἐκκλησία of Thessalonica. The ἐκκλησία mentioned here was composed of the βουλή and the δῆμος, and was a political body having authority to legislate for the city to which it belonged.

(2)   889

3   ὁρκίζω οὖν τὴν εὐλογημένην τῆς
          Ἀμφιπολιτῶν ἀγίας ἐκκλησίας ἐπισκοπὴν

The whole of this monumental inscription is extant. Only that portion of it is transcribed which is immediately concerned with the ἐκκλησία. It belongs to Amphipolis (l. 4). From the reference in it to the Trinity (ll. 3, 5) it is evidently a Christian inscription, but its exact date has not been ascertained. The translation of the whole of it is here given: "Having lived the common human life with grace and dignity, continually having made supplication to receive the hope of eternal life from the great and life-giving immaculate Trinity, I Liccon lie here. Therefore I adjure the blessed episcopate of the holy church of Amphipolis and the highly favored clergy by Father, by Son, and by Holy Spirit not to consent that any other person, in the future, be buried in this my burial-place."

The term ἐκκλησία here denotes the church. This usage is the one generally found in the New Testament, but rarely in the inscriptions. In this case it is implied that the ἐκκλησία has some authority over the burial-place, that it has power to grant or to withhold permission for burial in certain places.

Both of the usages found in the inscriptions for the term ἐκκλησία occur in the New Testament in widely different proportions. In one hundred and eleven occurrences of the word it is used one hundred and eight times with an ecclesiastical meaning, and only three times with

54   [270

the technical meaning, denoting a political body. In Acts 19:39 the word ἐκκλησία is used with reference to a body having authority to exercise judicial functions, and is referred to as an ἐκκλησία ἔννομος, that is, having legal authority and conducting its business within the requirements of the law. This ἐκκλησία ἔννομος is mentioned in contrast to the ἐκκλησία then assembled in the theater at Ephesus (Acts 19:32, 41), which was neither an ἐκκλησία κυρία, nor an ἐκκλησία σύγκλητος. That is, it was not one of the ordinary meetings of the ἐκκλησία, nor a specially called meeting, and so the γραμματεύς regarded it as an ἐκκλησία which had not conformed to the legal requirements for such an assembly. The people had assembled in the theater without being convened by any formal call, and disorder prevailed in the meeting.

In Acts 19:32, 41 the word ἐκκλησία denotes a political body, but implies that it was irregular in its proceedings, while in Acts 19:39 the reference is to the ἐκκλησία in its regular order of procedure. It is used with the technical meaning in both cases. Kennedy says, "In the New Testament the usage of the LXX determined the sense of the word, which is = the public gathering of Christians viewed externally as met for a common purpose, or organized with a common aim, or viewed from an inward standpoint as a spiritual corporation" (*Sources of N.T. Greek*, p. 99). To this classification of the usage of ἐκκλησία in the New Testament its usage in Acts 19:32, 39, 41 forms an important exception. The usage in this passage is not derived from the LXX, but from the usage common in Greek cities in that period. Such a usage was current in Ephesus where this event took place.

271

VIII.   κληρονόμος

(1)   180

7   Εἰ δὲ ὁ κληρονόμος ὁ ἐμὸς
           παραπέμψῃ τι, δώσει
           τῷ ταμιείῳ προστίμου δηνάρια ψν̄.

The whole of this inscription is extant, and the last three lines
are here transcribed, containing the term κληρονόμος. It belongs to
Thessalonica. Its date has not been ascertained.

According to this inscription a certain woman, Aurelia by name,
built a tomb for herself and her husband, and made this demand upon
her heir: "But if my heir neglect anything he shall pay to the treasurer
a fine of 750 denarii."

It appears that a testator had a right to impose certain obligations
upon the heir, and to fix a certain penalty for the violation of any such
conditions attaching to the inheritance.

(2)   262

26   (κληρ)ονόμων μου
         . . . ονων ἡ κληρο(νομία)

This inscription is found in a badly mutilated condition. The
whole of the left side of it is worn off, so that it is impossible to obtain
any adequate impression of the subject of it. It belongs to Deriopos.
Dimitsas thinks that it should be dated in the later Roman period,
γ′ . . . . δ′ αἰῶνα μ. X. (I, 307). Because of the words ὄρνιν and βωμόν
which occur in ll. 13 and 20, and which are associated with heathen forms
of worship, Dimitsas concludes that it was written before the introduction of Christianity into Deriopos.

If the restorations made above (ll. 26–27) be correct, there is mention
made of heirs and of an inheritance, but the context is so imperfect
that no information can be obtained concerning them.

(3)   402

           [ἐνορκίζω τοὺς κληρο-]
           νόμους μου πάν-
           τας τοὺς θεοὺς [ε]ἰς

                    56   [272

10   τὴν ληνὸν ταύτην
                ἕτερον μηδέν[α κοι-]
                μηθῆν[α]ι.

Only a portion of this inscription is preserved. The lines transcribed are from the middle of it, and contain the word under consideration. The inscription was found written upon a sarcophagus outside of the gate of Thessalonica. The date is not known.

According to this inscription a woman, while living, erected a temple and built a tomb for herself, and left the following injunction: "I adjure my heirs by all the gods not to bury any other body in this tomb." This is another example in which a solemn injunction is laid upon the heirs to keep the tomb of the deceased intact.

(4)   412
        Εἰ δέ τις τολμήσ[ε]ι ἀνοῖξ[αι], δώσ[ει] τοῖς
5   ἐμοῖς κληρονόμοις δηνάρια μύρια.

The whole of this inscription of five lines is extant, and the last two are transcribed. It belongs to Thessalonica. The exact date is not known, but from the Latin names (ll. 1-2) it apparently belongs sometime in the Roman period.

It reads thus: "Aurelia Marcia [built this tomb] for her dearest husband, the most noble Linius Aelius Nicostratus, from the common savings, for a memorial. If anyone shall dare to open it he shall pay to my heirs a thousand denarii."

The exceptional feature of this inscription is that the fine for disturbing the tomb of the deceased is to be paid to the heirs, not to the treasurer or to the city as was usual at that time. This indicates that the testator not only had the right to fix the amount of the fine to be paid for disturbing his tomb, but that he had it within his power to decide as to who should receive such money.

(5)   1220
        ε]ὖ εἰδὼς κληρονόμων τὴν ἐπιλησμοσύνην
5   καὶ κοινοῦ θανάτου μνημόσυνον προβλέπων

The whole of this inscription of eight lines is extant, and 4 and 5 are here transcribed. It was found in Thasos and belongs to the Roman period. It reads thus: "Aurelius Philip the son of Philip of Abdera while living built for himself and for his wife Antonia and for his children

273

[a tomb], well knowing the forgetfulness of heirs and foreseeing that his memory would be left behind by a common death. But if any other person wish to bury another body he shall pay to the city of Thasos two thousand denarii, and to the sacred treasurer two thousand denarii besides."

Whereas in many inscriptions of this kind a clause is inserted prohibiting others from using the tomb of the deceased and adding a penalty for the violation of this injunction, in this instance permission seems to be granted to bury another body in the same tomb by paying for the privilege or right. In the prohibitory clauses the fine is as high as 1,000 denarii for disturbing the tomb, but here the amount named is four thousand denarii. It is implied in this inscription that heirs were often remiss in the performance of their duties in memory of the deceased.

From these inscriptions it appears that certain obligations might be laid upon the heirs by the person bequeathing the inheritance, and that for failure to fulfil these conditions the heirs were subject to a fine, the amount of which was determined by the testator. Others also were liable to a fine for any desecration of a tomb. These fines were payable to the city, the sacred treasurer, or to the heirs as the testator directed. It seems to be implied, although not explicitly stated, that the persons on whom an obligation is laid always receive an inheritance.

In the New Testament the word κληρονόμος occurs fifteen times, with the same meaning, generically, as in the inscriptions.

Christians are called οἱ κληρονόμοι, "heirs of God" (Rom. 8:17), "heirs of the promise" (Heb. 6:17), "heirs of righteousness" (Heb. 11:7), "heirs of the kingdom" (Jas. 2:5). According to the New Testament, the basis of heirship is as follows: A son is an heir (Matt. 21:38; Mark 12:7; Luke 20:14; Heb. 1:2). All children (τέκνα) are heirs (Rom. 8:17). Abraham's seed are heirs (Gal. 3:29). Justification through the grace of Christ constitutes a man an heir (Tit. 3:7).

The fact that conditions attach to heirship is an element common to the inscriptions and the New Testament. In the latter every man might become an heir by complying with the conditions of the promise given to Abraham. In the inscriptions the one thing most often emphasized is the obligation of the κληρονόμος to fulfil certain conditions devolving upon him as heir. When Paul insists that only those who fulfil the conditions of heirship are truly heirs, he is making use of a well-known principle.

The objection that God does not die and cannot, therefore, have an heir, in any true sense of the word, arises from pressing the analogy too far. The Christian, who is spoken of as an heir, can assume the responsibilities of an heir and enter upon his inheritance without the death of God taking place. This is a question not raised by Paul, and it is a difficulty only to those who would press the comparison into details which are not pertinent to Paul's use of the term.

The two indispensable elements are: the assumption of certain responsibilities, and the receiving of an inheritance, on the part of the heir. These two elements are found both in the New Testament and in the inscriptions. The most important contribution which the inscriptions make at this point is in emphasizing the ancient idea of the right and authority of the person making the bequest to impose upon the heir certain conditions which he must fulfil.

IX.   κλῆρος

(1)   214

3   Τίκτε δ' ἐνὶ κλ[ήρ]οις Κερκείνιον.

The whole of this inscription of six lines is extant. It was found at Aiane, a town in the southern part of Macedonia, midway between the village of Kozane and the river Haliacmon. Its exact date is not known. The first three lines read thus: "Menedemos was the husband of Hadista, and Bouticos begot her. Aiane concealed her in death, but she was born in the fields of Circinium." In l. 3 the phrase, ἐνὶ κλήροις, is to be interpreted, "in the fields." (Cf. Dimitsas, Μακ., I, 223.) Liddell and Scott, under the term κλῆρος, cite Hdt. 9.24 in which the κλῆροι are called ἀγροί.

(2)   334
                        κλῆρον
                        ἐ]λευθ[ε]ροι

Of this inscription only the fragment transcribed above is preserved. It was found among the ruins of one of the churches in Achrida, but there is not enough of the context remaining by which to determine the meaning of κλῆρος.

(3)   889

                               ὁρκίζω οὖν,
              τὴν εὐλογημένην τῆς Ἀμφιπολιτῶν
              ἁγίας ἐκκλησίας ἐπισκοπὴν
5   καὶ τὸν ταύτης θεοφιλῆ κλῆρον

The whole of this inscription is extant. For its place and date, and a translation of it see VI. (2).

The author of this inscription solemnly adjures the blessed episcopate (ἐπισκοπήν) of the holy church of Amphipolis and the κλῆρον beloved of God not to consent that any other body shall be buried in his tomb. The meaning of the term κλῆρος which best suits this context is "the clergy," considered collectively. Examples of such usage are cited by Sophocles in his Greek Lexicon of the Roman and Byzantine periods.

60   [276

The cases referred to are all of a late date: Caius 29 B (A.D. 210); Petr. Alex. 448 B (A.D. 304); Anc. 3 (A.D. 314); Basil IV, 429 B (A.D.379); Greg. Naz. I. 1091 A (A.D. 390). Until we are able to determine the exact date of this inscription, it will be necessary to place it not earlier than the second century A.D., in order to give a sufficient length of time for the development of the episcopacy in the church. The meaning of κλῆρος in this inscription cannot be used as a proof that it was employed in this sense when the New Testament books were written. The usage of κλῆρος in this passage may, however, reflect an earlier usage.

In Goodspeed, *Index Patristicus*, the following occurrences of κλῆρος are given: Tral. 12:3; Bar. 6:6; *cit.* Rom. 1:2; Mar. 6:2; Diog. 12:9L; Eph. 11:2; Philad. 5:1. It is also found in Justin *Dial* 97:3; 113.3; *Apol.* 35.5, 8; 38.4; *Dial* 98.5; 104.1.

The word κλῆρος occurs eleven times in the New Testament with the following meanings:

1. It denotes the lot itself: Matt. 27:35; Mark 15:24; Luke 23:34; John 19:24; Acts 1:26.

2. It denotes the object assigned or allotted: (*a*) an allotment or office, Acts 1:17; (*b*) a portion or share, Acts 8:21; 26:18; (*c*) an inheritance or portion, Col. 1:12 (cf. Isaeus 6:56). In I Pet. 5:3, τῶν κλήρων should probably be classified under No. 2, but there is a lack of decisive evidence as to the specific meaning of this expression in I Peter.

Concerning the term κλῆρος the inscriptions, Nos. 214 and 889, seem to reflect a usage later than the time of the New Testament. In 889 κλῆρος has a distinctly ecclesiastical meaning as over against its legal significance in the New Testament. In the phrase ἐνὶ κλήροις the idea of its being an object assigned or allotted seems to have fallen into the background, and it is there used as a general designation for fields. Although in the New Testament κλῆρος is used of various objects, yet it is always with the idea that they have been allotted or assigned in a technical or legal sense.

X.   λειτουργέω, λειτουργία

(1)   247

. . . . . οἱ λειτουργείτωσαν, οἱ δὲ κεκτημένοι μόνον ταῖς τῇ
. . . . πιβαλλομέναις λειτουργίαις ὑπεύθυνοι ἔστωσαν τίνα
. . . τόπον στόρνυσθαι τὰς ὁδοὺς κοινῷ διατάγματι ἐδήλωσα
. . λεύω καὶ ἀντανοὺς συντελεῖν ὑμεῖν εἰς τὰ ἀναλώματα
5 τὸ τρίτον συνεισφέροντας, ἡ δὲ συνεισφορὰ γενέσθω ἀπὸ
τῶν ἐν Μακεδονίᾳ ὄντων ἀντανῶν εὐτυχεῖτε.

Most of this inscription is preserved, as here transcribed. It is seen that the upper left hand corner is worn, or broken off. It was found near Bitolia, in the district of Lyncestis in Macedonia. Dimitsas thinks that it belongs to the Macedonian era, before the time of the Roman dominion (Μακ., I, 272).

The verb λειτουργείτωσαν occurs in l. 1, but owing to the fact that the upper left-hand corner is broken off, it is not known who performed the services. Dimitsas suggests the following possible restorations for the beginning of this line: "οἱ μὲν νόμοι" ἡ "οἱ μὲν ἄποροι."

In l. 2 the dative plural of λειτουργία occurs.

The services referred to here consisted in the leveling of the ways or roads. The owners or masters (κεκτημένοι) were responsible for these public services. This tends to show that certain persons in the community were under obligation to perform such services for the public. This view is confirmed by a passage in Isaeus (7:5) in which three men possessing large estates were required to λειτουργεῖν for the city. Cf. Dem. 833:26. Thus the λειτουργία does not seem always to have been a matter of voluntary contribution. In some cases, at least, it appears to have been obligatory.

(2)   1131

2   ἀγορανομήσας καὶ ἐν
ταῖς ἄλλαις ἀρχαῖς καὶ λειτοργίαις
ἐπιφανῶς πολιτευσάμενος

The whole of this inscription is extant, and that portion of it which contains the word under consideration is here transcribed. It was found in Thasos, and probably belongs to the Roman period. It reads as follows: "Aurelius Herodotus the son of Paranomus twice was chief of the magistrates, held the office of ἀγορανόμος, and with other offices and services he distinguished himself as a citizen, living seventy-five years. Farewell beloved" (ll. 1–5).

The λειτουργίαι are referred to here as a part of the means by which Herodotus gained for himself distinction as a citizen. The context suggests that the services were voluntary on the part of Herodotus, but there is no indication as to what these services were.

A parallel to the usage of these terms is found in the New Testament. The verb λειτουργέω occurs three times, and the noun λειτουργία seven times, with the following usages: to denote services rendered (1) on behalf of the poor at Jerusalem; (2) to the Lord; (3) on behalf of Paul, in personal ministration to his needs; (4) on behalf of the people, through the priestly office.

In Rom. 15:27 the service is obligatory. In this passage the idea of obligation to perform the services seems to be moral rather than civic or legal as in 247.

In the Scriptures these terms seem to be associated with religious services, and generally with the priestly function. In the inscriptions this religious or sacerdotal aspect of the services does not appear. Generically the terms have the same meaning in the New Testament as in the inscriptions, but specifically they are used with reference to different kinds of services. The idea that the λειτουργίαι are services rendered on behalf of the people is common to both.

XI.   νόμος

(1)   349

Μο. σης ὁ Γρηγόριος [ταύτη]ν Θ(ε)ῷ σκηνὴν ἐγείρας τὸν θεόγραφον νόμον
ἔθνη τὰ Μυσῶν ἐκδιδάσκει πανσόφως. Ἔτεισωκ.

The whole of this inscription is extant and is here transcribed.
It was found in a church in Achrida, Macedonia, and belongs to the
year 1312 A.D., at which time this church was rebuilt by Gregory.
It reads: "Gregory, having erected this tabernacle to God, teaches
all-wisely the nations of the Mysians the divinely written law."

The νόμος is described as θεόγραφος, thus indicating that it is
thought of as a written law and as coming from God. The date of
this inscription is so late that this usage of νόμος cannot be cited as
evidence for the usage of νόμος in the first century A.D. It is, however,
interesting to observe that the usage of νόμος which is found here is
the one most common in the New Testament, where, with two excep-
tions, it occurs in the singular number, generally denoting a body of
statutes.

(2)   666

Αἱ μὲν δοθεῖσαι τῷ θεόπτῃ πρὶν πλάκες.
2   νόμους σκιώδεις εἶχον ἐγγεγραμμένους.

The whole of this inscription is extant, except parts of the last
two lines. It was found in a Greek church in Thessalonica, and the
lines transcribed read as follows: "The tablets given aforetime to the
seer had shadowy laws written on them."

The plural, νόμους, which occurs in l. 2 denotes individual statutes.
This usage of the term νόμος is quite exceptional in the New Testament,
being found only in Heb. 8:10; 10:16, out of one hundred and ninety-
five occurrences of the word. There being but two instances of νόμος
in the inscriptions, we should not be justified in entering into an extended
comparison of the word in the New Testament. As already noted,
the two usages of the inscriptions find a parallel in the New Testament,
one of the two being quite unusual in the New Testament, while the
other is the one most commonly found there.

XII.   πολιτάρχης

For an exhaustive treatment of the term πολιτάρχης see *The Politarchs in Macedonia and Elsewhere*, by Ernest DeWitt Burton.

Brief mention will here be made concerning the functions of the πολιτάρχαι, and their relationship to the βουλή or governing body of the city in which they held office. In the Macedonian inscriptions the noun πολιτάρχης occurs seven times (217:24, 36, 40; 258:5; 675:2, 48; 738:4), and the verb πολιταρχέω ten times (2:2; 248:6; 260:3; 364:1; 365:10; 366:7; 367:13; 368:1; 683:4; 886:4).

In 248 the office of πολιτάρχης is mentioned as one of several offices successively held by a certain man in the city of Lyncestis. This man held the office of πολιτάρχης and of ταμίας at the same time. The πολιτάρχαι are represented as being subject to the command of the βουλή and the δῆμος (248, 258, 365, etc.). In Idranizi a δόγμα was passed by the πολιτάρχης and the πολῖται, and on the same occasion the πολιτάρχης was enjoined to see that the δόγμα was enforced (217). The text is deficient at this point, but it appears as if the πολιτάρχης were subject to a double fine (to the imperial treasury and to the city) if he should in any way attempt to set aside the δόγμα which had been enacted.

It thus appears that the πολιτάρχης was an officer of prominence in the city, and that he exercised both legislative and executive functions. In Tzepikobon the πολιτάρχαι assembled the βουλευτήριον (258:5). In Lete they introduced the προβούλευμα in the ἐκκλησία. The πολιτάρχαι and the treasurer of the city were commanded by the βουλή and the δῆμος to inscribe the decree and erect the stele (675:2, 46). In 365 the πολιτάρχαι are associated with the ἀρχιερεύς and both are subject to the command of the βουλή. On this occasion the πολιτάρχαι were the officers delegated to see that the decree was executed.

This is of special significance to us because it occurred in Thessalonica where Jason and the brethren were brought before the πολιτάρχαι (Acts 17:6–8) who seem to have been acting in a capacity similar to that of the πολιτάρχαι mentioned in the inscriptions. In the inscriptions as in the Acts passage they appear as executive officers, a part of whose duties was to see that the laws were enforced. It appears then that the only mention of the πολιτάρχαι in the New Testament pertains to a Macedonian city, and that they were executive officers subject to the βουλή or governing body of the city. They were responsible for the maintenance of order and the enforcement of the law in accordance with the statutes of the city in which they held office. In Thessalonica they were associated with the ἀρχιερεύς and probably were subordinate in authority to him (365).

XIII.   πραιτώριον
(1)   281

Τι(βέριον) Κλαύδιον Φόρτιον, Οὐετρανὸν
στρατευσάμενον ἐν πραιτωρίῳ

For place and date and translation of this inscription see III. (3).
Only a part of it is extant.

It is here asserted that Tiberius Claudius served as a soldier ἐν
πραιτωρίῳ. The word πραιτώριον is simply a transliteration of the
Latin word *praetorium,* and is not found in the Greek earlier than the
first century A.D. To understand the meaning of this term in Greek
it may be necessary to consider its usage in Latin. The following are
the various possible meanings which have been assigned to it in the Latin.

1. The tent of a general (Liv. 10:33).
2. The official residence of the governor of a province (Tertull.
ad Scap. § 3; Cic. *Verr.* 2, 4, § 28).
3. Any spacious villa or palace (Plut. *Tib.* 39; Juv. *Sat.* 1:75).
4. The camp of the praetorian guard (Pitiscus, *Thesaur. antiq.* iii.
174; Tac. *Ann.* 4. 2).
5. The praetorian guard itself (*CIL*, 3365).
6. The residence of the emperor at Baiae (cf. *Hermes,* IV, 102, l. 2).

In the lines transcribed above (281:2) the term πραιτώριον must
come under either No. 4 or 5, as the context seems to exclude the other
meanings. From the Latin inscriptions it is seen that the phrase,
miles in praetorio (*CIL*, 5777), refers to the soldiers of the praetorian
guard, and *militavit in praetorio* (*CIL*, 7328) is precisely analogous
to the expression στρατευσάμενον ἐν πραιτωρίῳ. The Latin phrase
means that he served as a soldier in the praetorian guard. There is
then a strong probability that ἐν πραιτωρίῳ refers to the praetorian
guard rather than to the camp.

(2)   282

Τι(βέριος) Κλαύδιος 'Ροῦφος Οὐ-
ετρανὸς ἐκ πραιτω-
ρίου δράκοντι τῷ
ὧδε τειμω-
5   μένῳ
283]   67

The whole of this inscription is extant and is here transcribed.   It was found between Plethar and Troïak and belongs to the same period as the preceding one.   It reads: "Tiberius Claudius Rufus a veteranus of the praetorium to the serpent which is here honored."

Here again the Latin inscriptions throw light upon the interpretation of the phrase ἐκ πραιτωρίου.   The phrase *veteranus ex praetorio* occurs six times (*CIL*, 3365, 5412, 5505, 7596, 10198, 10286).   Here it is used of a veteran of the praetorian guard.   Following this analogy the phrase, ἐκ πραιτωρίου, seems to indicate that Tiberius was a member of the praetorian guard.   It denotes the soldiers themselves, and not their place of encampment.

This usage of the term in the Latin and in the Macedonian Greek inscriptions affords some light on a much-disputed passage in the New Testament.

In Phil. 1:13 there has been much controversy as to the meaning of πραιτώριον.   Meyer and others contend that it refers to the camp or barracks of the praetorian guard, while Lightfoot, with many others, maintains that it refers to the praetorian guard itself.   While the inscriptions do not furnish conclusive proof on this question, they tend to sustain the interpretation of Lightfoot in rendering it "praetorian guard."

It should be observed as against Meyer in his *Commentary on Phil.* (4th ed. of the German) that so far as the word itself is concerned or its then current usage, it is not impossible that it might be used with reference to the residence of the emperor.   See the edict of Claudius in the year 46 A.D.

> Bais in praetorio edictum
> Ti Claudi Caesaris Augusti Germanici propositum fuit
> id quod infra scriptum est.

This edict of Claudius was issued at the town of Baiae "in praetorio," that is in the residence or palace of the emperor at Baiae (cf. Mommsen, *Hermes*, IV, 102).   For the fact that the emperors had villas or palaces at Baiae consult Varr. *R. R.*, iii. 17. 9; Seneca *Ep.* 51; Tac. *Ann.* xiv. 9.

XIV.   πρεσβεύω, πρεσβεία, πρεσβευτής, πρεσβύτερος

A.   πρεσβεύω

(1)   248

2   πρεσβεύσας εἰς Δελφοὺς ἐπὶ τὸν Πύθιον,

The whole of this inscription is extant, but only the line containing
the word under consideration is here transcribed. From l. 7 we learn
that it belongs to some city in Lyncestis.

Beginning at the middle of l. 2 it reads: "Paulus Calidius having
gone as an envoy to Delphi to consult the oracle, having furnished
money to the city for the purchase of corn, having purchased corn in
a time of want, having been gymnasiarch at his own expense, while
holding the office of treasurer and of politarch, having been esteemed
worthy by a decree of the council of the setting up of images and of
life-size statues, and while he was gymnasiarch being appointed a son
of the city both by the city and by the nation of Lyncestis, set up the
stele at his own expense."

This official visit as an envoy to Delphi is mentioned, among other
good deeds, as something of distinction, reflecting honor on the memory
of this man. While the object of his mission is not explicitly stated,
it is implied that he went there to consult the oracle on some matter
of interest to the public.

(2)   330
                    Ἀγαθῇ τύχῃ.
                 Δασσαρήτιοι Δρύ-
                 αντα Κα[ι]πίωνος
                 τὸ]ν προστάτην
5   π]ρεσβεύσαντα
                 πρὸς] τὸν κύριον
                 Αὐτ]οκράτορα
                    .   .   .   .

The portion of this inscription which is extant is here transcribed.
It was found in Achrida. It reads: "With good luck. The Dasseretae
[honor] Druas the son of Caepio the chief who went an envoy to the
lord emperor . . . ."

The name of the person to whom the envoy was sent is broken off. The object of his mission is not mentioned, but he was evidently acting in a political capacity, going as an envoy for the Dasseretae to some emperor. The verb πρεσβεύω is here used in a technical sense, denoting an official action.

(3)

The word ἐπρεσβ(ε)ύσ(αντ)ο occurs in inscription 370, which was found in Thessalonica, but the ends of all the lines are broken off, so that the inscription is wholly unintelligible.

The verb πρεσβεύω has the same technical meaning in the New Testament as in the inscriptions. It occurs only in II Cor. 5:20 and Eph. 6:20, where Paul uses it in a figurative sense of himself as an envoy of Christ. Here as in the inscriptions it denotes official action of a representative. This usage of πρεσβεύω throws some light on how Paul thought of himself as related to Christ in his work as a preacher of the gospel.

B.   πρεσβεία

(1)   37

                    ἐλέησον ἡμᾶς ὡς
5   υἱο(ὺ)ς αὐτοῦ πρεσβ[ε]ίαις καὶ εὐχαῖς π[άντων
       ἀγγέλων [καὶ] προφητῶν

For the place, date, and translation of this inscription see I. A. (2). The term πρεσβείαις (l. 5) is co-ordinate with εὐχαῖς and is used in a prayer, evidently denoting intercessions.

(2)

The accusative singular of the noun πρεσβεία occurs in a fragment of an inscription (253) found in the region of Moglia, to the north of Bitolia, but there is not sufficient context extant to enable us to determine what the inscription was about. There is then only one occurrence of πρεσβεία in the inscriptions in which its meaning is clear to us.

The usage which we have found in 37 has no parallel in the New Testament. The word occurs in Luke 14:32 and 19:14. In Luke 14:32 one king sends a πρεσβεία to another king to ask him for peace. In 19:14 the πολῖται send a πρεσβεία to their own ruler. This usage of πρεσβεία is in accord with that of the corresponding verb, πρεσβεύω, in the inscriptions.

C.   πρεσβευτής

(1)   217

45   τοῦτο τὸ δόγμα ἔ-
            δοξε τῷ διέποντι τὴν ἐπαρ-
            χίαν Ἰουνίῳ Ῥουφίνῳ διὰ
            τῶν πρεσβευτῶν τοῦ . . . . .

For the place and date of this inscription see IV. (2). The whole
of the inscription is extant in a somewhat fragmentary condition. The
part transcribed above reads: "this decree is decreed by Junius Rufinus
who is governing the eparchy by the πρεσβευταί."

As respects the πρεσβευταί they are acting in an official capacity,
and are subordinate to Rufinus the governor. They are executive
officers under the authority of the governor. Their office seems here
to have more or less of permanency. It is not limited to a single event,
and in this respect it is more closely related to the conception of the
office of πρεσβευτής which Paul had when he called himself an ambassador of Christ.

(2)   671

36   ἀποστεῖλαι δὲ καὶ πρεσβυτήν

                · · · · · · · · · ·

45   πρεσβευτὴς εἱρέθη Τυννωνος.

                · · · · · · · · · ·

48   παρ' ὑμῶν ἀποσταλέντος πρεσβευτοῦ

                · · · · · · · · · ·

58   ἀποσταλεὶς πρεσβευτὴς πρὸς τὴν πόλιν

                · · · · · · · · · ·

The whole of this inscription is extant, but only the phrases containing the term πρεσβευτής are here transcribed. For its place and
date, and a translation of it see I. A. (9).

The word πρεσβευτής occurs four times, referring in each case to
the same man. Boulon was appointed a πρεσβευτής by the δῆμος of
Delos (l. 57), to go to Thessalonica on a specific mission. He was
received in Thessalonica in the ἐκκλησία, and was permitted to present
to that body the matters contained in the decree. Having accomplished
his purpose, he returned to Delos with the answer of the ἐκκλησία.
He was not merely an official messenger whose duty ended with the
delivery of the document in his charge. He endeavored to present his
cause in as persuasive a manner as possible and so win the approval
and co-operation of the ἐκκλησία.

Only one πρεσβευτής was sent on this occasion. The number of men commissioned on an embassy was variable. In 675 there are three, and probably also in 217.

(3)   675
40   ἐλέσθαι δὲ καὶ πρεσβευτάς
    .   .   .   .

49   καὶ εἱρέθησαν πρεσβευταὶ τῶν βουλευτῶν
    .   .   .   .

The whole of this inscription is extant, but only the phrases containing the word under consideration are transcribed. For its place and date see I. A. (10).

In this instance the πρεσβευταί were chosen from the members of the βουλή, and were three in number. They were chosen by the βουλή and the δῆμος and were commissioned to convey to the Roman treasurer the decree of honor passed on his behalf, and to urge upon him the acceptance of the honor.

The noun πρεσβευτής is not found in the New Testament in this form, but πρεσβύτης in Philem., vs. 9, is apparently the same word, with this slight variation in spelling. In the original inscriptions as in the original text of the New Testament, the words are without accent, and would appear thus, πρεσβευτης and πρεσβυτης. The interchange of ευ and υ in Greek orthography is of common occurrence. So far then as the accent and the orthography are concerned, there is no reason for making a distinction between πρεσβευτής in the inscriptions and πρεσβύτης in Philem., vs. 9. See Hort., N.T., Vol. II, Appendix, p. 136.

The πρεσβευταί seem to have been chosen from men of influence, as in Lete, from members of the βουλή. They were representative officers and generally were appointed for some particular purpose pertaining to the welfare of the people.

In the Epistle to Philemon when Paul designates himself as πρεσβύτης it is under circumstances similar to that under which the πρεσβευταί of the inscriptions held office. According to Paul's own statement he is in the act of pleading for Onesimus when he uses this title of himself. Orthography and accent are variable and cannot in this instance be used as an argument to show that πρεσβύτης has a different meaning from that of πρεσβευτής. It seems then to be clear that ambassador is a possible interpretation of πρεσβύτης in Philemon, or rather, that πρεσβύτης ("old man") is a transcriptional error for πρεσβευτής.

D.   πρεσβύτερος

(1)   110
           Μημόριον Εὐγενίου
           πρεσβυτέρου

(2)   111
           Μημόριον
           Θεοδούλου κ[αὶ
           Εὐτροπίου πρεσβυτέρου.

The whole of each of these inscriptions is extant, and is here transcribed. They were found in Beroea. The Latin word μημόριον for μνημεῖον, and the word Θεόδουλος both point to a late date for this inscription, probably as late as the first century A.D.

It does not seem possible in these inscriptions to decide whether πρεσβύτερος is used as a noun or as an adjective. It may be used here as an official designation, or it may be an adjective referring to age.

(3)   1324
           Παίστρατος Κτησιφῶντος πρεσβύτε[ρος
           Παίστρατος Κτησιφῶντος
           νεώτερος.

The whole of this inscription is extant and is here transcribed. It was found in Thasos.

From the manifest antithesis of πρεσβύτερος and νεώτερος it is evident that both words refer to age. Two men of the same name, Παίστρατος, are distinguished by terms denoting their relative ages.

A striking parallel to this usage of πρεσβύτερος is found in I Tim. 5:1, 2, and in I Pet. 5:5. Alford, Kühl, and von Soden take πρεσβύτερος in these passages as referring to official position and not to age. The above inscription affords us an example of these two words, πρεσβύτερος and νεώτερος, used in contrast to each other where both words refer to age. This tends to sustain those who interpret πρεσβύτερος with reference to age in the scripture passages.

The almost universal usage of πρεσβύτερος in the New Testament is as an official designation. For an excellent discussion as to the origin of this technical usage see Deissmann, *Bible Studies*, pp. 154–57, 233–35. This official usage was common in Egypt, and in all probability in Asia Minor before the first century A.D. (Cf. *Flind. Petr.*, *Pap.*, II, iv, 6, 13²; *CIG*, 1417).

XV   στρατηγός

(1)   346

                     Φίλιππος Μουν-
5   τανοῦ ἀνέθηκαν
                     στρατηγῷ Νικίᾳ.

The whole of this inscription of six lines is extant, and the last
three are here transcribed. It was found near Lake Lychnidos in Macedonian Illyria. It reads as follows: "Epicadus the son of Genthius
and Philip the son of Mountanus set up [this monument] to Nicias
a στρατηγός."

Only one man is mentioned as holding the office of στρατηγός, and
nothing is said as to his functions. This inscription seems to have
been inscribed to his memory by private individuals rather than by
the city.

(2)
The word στρατηγός occurs in inscriptions 622, 630, 631, 649, 650,
651, and 660. They were found at Thessalonica and belong to the
ninth century A.D., which is too late to be of value in this investigation.
At this late date the office seems to have been held by but one man,
and to have pertained to a city or province: that is, it was political.

(3)   675

12   ἐφ᾽ οὓς καὶ ἐκπορευθέ[ντ]ος Σέξτου
                     Πομπηΐου τοῦ στρατηγοῦ καὶ παραταξαμένου
                     μετὰ τ]ῶν ἰδίων στρατιωτῶν.

The whole of this large inscription of fifty lines is extant. The
portion transcribed illustrates the usage of στρατηγός. For the place
and date of this inscription see I. A. (10).

The word στρατηγός is here a military term, applied to the well-
known Sextus Pompeius, general of the army.

The inscription is in honor of Marcus Annius the Roman treasurer,
and in recounting the favors which he had done for the city of Lete,
and the enemies against whom he had fought in their behalf, reference
is here made to certain enemies, "against whom also Sextus Pompeius
the στρατηγός went forth, and drew up in battle order with his own
soldiers."

                     74   [290

(4)

Reference is made to the στρατηγός of Thessalonica in inscriptions, 711, 714, 715, 716, and 717, but nothing is said as to the duties of his office.

It appears then that the term στρατηγός is used to designate (1) a military officer, (2) an officer of a city, (3) an officer of a province. The third sense is common in papyri.

Unfortunately most of the inscriptions in which the στρατηγός is mentioned are very brief, and no reference is made in them to his functions, except in the case of Sextus Pompeius. With this one exception the form of the title seems to indicate that the office of στρατηγός pertained to civic or political matters, rather than to military. It was not a title limited to the designation of one particular office. In this respect its use here is similar to that of στρατηγός in the New Testament.

The word is used only by Luke. It occurs seven times in the plural number (Luke 22:4, 52; Acts 16:20, 22, 35, 36, 38), and three times in the singular number (Acts 4:1; 5:24, 26). In Acts 5:26 the στρατηγός of the temple goes with the ὑπηρέται to make an arrest. In Luke 22:55 the στρατηγοί of the temple are among those who come to arrest Jesus. In the sixteenth chapter of Acts the στρατηγοί of Philippi exercise judicial functions. The κύριοι of a slave girl led Paul and Silas to the στρατηγοί of the city for judgment. The στρατηγοί had authority to beat, imprison, or set free, except in the case of Roman citizens who could demand a formal trial.

In Latin the corresponding term *praefectus* is used in the same manner as στρατηγός in the inscriptions. In neither case is the term limited to the designation of a particular office. The functions pertaining to the various offices were specific, but the term denoting the office was general. This will account for the use of the word στρατηγός in the New Testament, in referring to men holding different kinds of offices.

XVI. ταμιεῖον

(1)   180

7
> Εἰ δὲ ὁ κληρονόμος ὁ ἐμὸς
> παραπέμψῃ τι, δώσει
> τῷ ταμιείῳ προστίμου δηνάρια ψν.

The whole of this inscription of nine lines is extant, but only the last three lines are transcribed. For its place and date see VII. (1).

A certain woman erected a tomb for herself and husband and made this provision: "but if my heir pass over anything he shall pay to the treasury a fine of 750 denarii."

It is clear that ταμιεῖον here denotes the treasury, in all probability the treasury of the city.

(2)   413

4
> δώσ[ε]ι τῷ τα[μ]ιείῳ *φ.

Only the latter portion of this inscription is preserved, and only a part of the last line is transcribed.

The extant portion reads: "but if any one, having opened the tomb, dare to bury another without the consent of my wife, he shall pay to the treasury five hundred denarii." It belongs to Thessalonica. The date has not been ascertained. Money is to be paid to the ταμιεῖον, that is, to the treasury.

(3)   420

3
> εἰ δὲ μ[ή, δ]ώσ[ε]ι τῷ ταμ[ε]ίῳ ὑπὲρ ἑκάστη[ς] ληνοῦ * . . . .

Only a small fragment of this inscription is preserved. It was found in Thessalonica. The part transcribed is the only intelligible statement in the extant portion. Reference is here made to the payment of a certain sum of money to the ταμιεῖον.

(4)   426

5
> δώσει τῷ [ἱε]ρωτάτῳ ταμείῳ προστείμου * μυ.

The whole of this inscription of five lines is extant, and the last line is here transcribed. It was found in Thessalonica.

A husband and wife built for themselves a tomb and made this provision: "but whoever dares to bury any other person besides those added in writing, he shall pay to the most sacred treasury a fine of 440 denarii."

(5)   447
3   δώσει τῷ κυριακῷ ταμείῳ
              δηνάρια πέντε χιλιάδας.

The whole of this inscription of four lines is extant, but only the last clause of it is transcribed. It was found at Kalamaria near Thessalonica. It reads: "Gaius Julius Eutychus, while living, built this tomb for himself, and if any person, after I am buried, open it and bury another, he shall pay to the imperial treasury 5,000 denarii." This reference to the imperial treasury shows that the inscription belongs to some time in the imperial period.

(6)   740
8   δώσει τῷ ἱερωτάτῳ ταμ[ε]ίῳ
              * μύρια

The whole of this inscription is extant, but only the last two lines are transcribed. It was found in Sokho which lies between Thessalonica and Sirrhae. Dimitsas dates it about the first or second century A.D. (Μακ., II, 602).

A certain man, Dionysius, erected a tomb for his son and provided that if any other person should use this tomb for burial, he must pay to the most sacred treasury 12,000 denarii.

(7)   781
4   δώσει προστείμου τῷ ταμείῳ * ,β καὶ τῇ πόλει ,β.

The whole of this inscription of five lines is extant, and the fourth line is transcribed. The inscription was found in Amphipolis, and belongs to the year 205 A.D.

A certain man built a tomb for himself and his wife and on it he wrote the following: "And if any other man shall dare to open [this tomb], or to bury another body in it, he shall pay a fine to the treasury of 10,000 denarii, and to the city 12,000 denarii." In this case the ταμιεῖον does not refer to the treasury of the city, as one fine is paid to the ταμιεῖον and one to the city.

293

(8)   829

Ἔστιν γε καὶ ἐπὶ τῇ τῶν
ἀνθρώπων σωτηρίᾳ τὸ τοιοῦτο καὶ ἐπὶ τοῦ ἱερωτάτου ταμείου
15   ις ὠφελείᾳ.

The whole of this inscription containing eighty-seven lines is preserved, except the first eight lines of it.   Beginning at the middle of
l. 13 a line and a half is transcribed above.

In this inscription a protest is made against certain unjust practices
of the ruling classes in oppressing the common people, and it is asked
not only that their demands be granted, but that they be inscribed
and set up in some public place.   In support of their protest they say
in the lines transcribed above: "Such a thing is for the safety of men
and for the advantage of the sacred treasury."   In this instance the
interests of the sacred treasury are closely associated with the welfare
of men in general.

(9)   1220

7   οὗτος δώσει τῇ Θασίων πόλει δηνάρια B̄
           καὶ τῷ ἱερωτάτῳ ταμείῳ ἄλλα δηνάρια B̄.

The whole of this inscription is extant, and the last two lines are
here transcribed.   For its place and date, and a translation of it see
VII. (5).

In this inscription, as in 781 above, money is to be paid both to the
ταμιεῖον and to the city.

This dissertation presupposes that we no longer regard the Greek
of the New Testament as an isolated language.   Its sources are to be
found in (1) the Greek inscriptions, (2) the non-literary Greek papyri
of Egypt, (3) the current Greek literature of that period, (4) the Septuagint.   In these four sources there is essential unity, with some
slight variations.

The Septuagint is in "translation Greek."   It is the Greek in common
use at that time, with some modifications in construction conforming
to the Hebrew idioms which it translated.   Ideas and concepts appeared
in the Hebrew Scriptures which were foreign to the Greeks, and so
new Greek words, in some cases at least, were formed to express these
new concepts.   In other instances familiar Greek words were used
with a different shade of meaning.

In the non-literary Greek papyri the language of everyday life is used. Many private letters have been found which preserve for us the vernacular of the common people.

As respects inscriptions they were scattered over the whole area of the Greek-speaking world, and are an important factor in showing that the Greek spoken throughout the Roman empire was in the main homogeneous. While they were written in the Greek then current, they are probably farther removed from the spoken language than are the non-literary Greek papyri. The inscriptions were intended for the public, and so were more formal, more nearly in accord with the literary usage of the time, than were the personal letters found in the papyri. They were for the most part of a legal or technical character, and so were expressed in a more formal manner than the spoken language.

The prose literature of that period might be taken as a sufficient source for the New Testament Greek, were it not that it seems to be pretty well established that writers of the New Testament drew more largely from the oral language of the common people than did such writers as Polybius, Josephus, or Philo. In this respect a closer parallel to the Greek of the New Testament is to be found in the Greek papyri. A wider range of usage may be obtained from the inscriptions than from a single writer.

This treatise is concerned with only one of these sources, the Greek inscriptions, and that from a definite geographical area. The inscriptions from Macedonia are rather intimately related to the writings of the New Testament. Some of the first gentile Christian churches were founded in Macedonia. Some of the first epistles written by Paul were to churches in Macedonia. Most of these inscriptions belong to the time in which the κοινή was the current language, and are themselves written in this "common" Greek.

In view of these facts it is evident that any lexical research in the field of the inscriptions will have a bearing upon the language of the New Testament. Those inscriptions which contain legal and governmental terms are in the very nature of the case connected with official business, and such terms have almost invariably a strictly technical meaning in the inscriptions. In the New Testament these legal and governmental terms are generally used in a figurative sense, in religious phraseology. It is not therefore to be supposed that there will be an exact parallelism of usage in these two fields, but their figurative usage in the New Testament depends for its significance upon the strictly technical meaning assigned to the terms in literature which is manifestly intended to be official and technical. In this respect it is hoped that this investigation may, in some measure, make a contribution toward a better understanding of the writings of the New Testament, and that the word-index will be of value to all those who desire to make further investigations in the field of the Macedonian inscriptions.

INDEX OF THE MACEDONIAN INSCRIPTIONS

404:2; 463:4; 466:4;
514:1; 687:3; 1081:1;
1411:8
ἐαυτῷ, 78:6; 80:2; 106:4;
205:4; 263:2; 283:2;
287:3; 399:2; 406:3;
418:1; 429:2; 434:2;
436:8; 447:1; 454:3;
462:5; 471:6; 475:4;
483:3; 488:4; 494:4;
522:1; 815:2; 817:2;
845:6; 1220:2; 1298:1
ἐαυτῇ, 161:2; 179:6;
287:5; 390:3; 402:2;
427:2; 431:6; 444:5;
445:4; 449:5; 459:1;
465:6; 499:3; 509:1;
531:1; 691:5; 818:4;
845:3; 874:3
ἐαυτόν, 82:4; 99:3; 675:16
ἐαυτήν, 260:5
ἐαυτῶν, 395:3; 746:5;
813:7; 1412:6
ἐαυτοῖς, 204:2; 217:10;
387:7; 394:1; 414:2;
417:1; 419:4; 426:2;
435:9; 455:3; 456:2;
493:5; 495:3; 496:3;
863:12
ἐαυτούς, 281:7
ἐγείρει, 112:1
ἤγειρε, 611:2
ἤγειρεν, 1417:9
ἐγείρας, 349:1
ἐγγόνῳ, 409:2
ἐγγόνοις, 394:1
ἐγκλημάτων, 112:1
ἐγκαταλιπεῖν, 829:39
ἐγκατέχει, 1140:2
ἐγκώμιον, 240:1
ἔδαφος, 5:4
ἔδει, 360:3
ἔδη, 361:6
ἔδρα, 362:1
ἔδρ’, 361:4
θέλητε, 208:6
ἠθέλησεν, 258:25
θελέτω, 1369:8

ἔθνους, 248:7; 675:11
ἔθνη, 349:2
ἔθος, 1380:7
ἔθου, 670:10
ἔθ’, 361:7
ἔθει, 370:21
εἰ, 83:2; 180:7; 198:51;
370:8; 420:2; 855:
17; 1172:5; 1369:1;
1417:6
εἰδέ, 412:4
εἰδήμονα, 1122:1
εἰδῆτε, 671:54
εἴδειν, 398:4
εἰδότες, 403:11
εἰδέναι, 365:6
εἰκοστῷ, 410:1
εἰκοστόν, 1163:3
εἰκόνων, 248:4
εἰμή, 829:54
εἰμή, 361:4
ἐστί, 397:4; 498:6
ἐστ’, 5:4
ἐστιν, 255:13; 397:5;
764:4; 829:13, 53, 71;
1140:3
εἰσί, 976:57
ἤν, 4:3; 116:3; 1364:4, 8
ἔστω, 200:4; 203:10, 13;
742:9; 847:22; 1130:
13; 1369:12
ἔστων, 1369:6, 9
εἶναι, 125:10; 198:9,
49, 60; 255:17, 22;
829:38, 69; 847:11,
976:15, 29, 45; 1130:6;
1364:5, 6
ἐών, 909:4
ἐώντων, 198:38
ὤν, 1130:4
ὄντος, 593:6
ἔην, 214:1
ἦεν, 329:8
ὄντα, 671:38, 73
ὄντας, 255:15
ἐόντας, 1364:8
ἔσκε, 401:2
ἐσσομένοισι, 76:7

ἴη, 742:A', 6
εἰν, 363:4
εἴνεκεν, 401:3; 829:25
εἰρήνηι, 675:33
εἰς, 46:9; 173:2; 217:28,
42; 248:2, 3; 255:8, 10,
19; 258:23; 279:6; 329:2;
353:5; 396:4; 419:6;
607:1; 612:2, 4; 671:15,
16, 17, 18, 29, 30, 35, 37,
50, 60; 672:4; 675:11,
20, 44, 45; 740:5; 743:9;
749:9; 764:6; 787:2;
829:22, 27, 41, 55, 76,
78, 83; 1108:4; 1110:6;
1130:6, 11; 1334:3;
1369:16; 1417:10
ἐς, 195:3; 198:25; 360:
5; 847:16; 909:7;
976:10, 38, 40, 41, 52,
59; 1369:18; 1419:6
εἰσάγοντι, 763:29
εἰσενέθηκεν, 5:8
εἰσέλαχεν, 160:9
εἰσφέρει, 666:4
εἴτε, 198:6
εἴως, 1369:12
ἐκ, 16:4; 29:5; 62:5;
80:1; 87:1; 143:4; 149:2;
179:4; 180:2; 181:3;
198:1; 213:4; 222:7;
231:5; 248:4, 8; 258:12,
21; 260:5; 261:3; 282:2;
294:4; 299:7; 300:6;
352:2; 355:1; 363:(5),
3; 365:7; 369:6; 380:3;
403:6; 411:2; 412:3;
417:1; 419:5; 426:2;
429:3; 462:4; 463:3;
475:3; 476:2; 499:2;
536:6; 550:1; 560:2;
593:1; 611:3; 668:4;
675:31; 740:3; 764:4,
6; 786:4; 804:3; 811:7;
909:7; 927:4; 976:18,
20; 1069:2; 1080:3;
1085:3; 1087:1; 1089:3;
1130:8; 1135:3; 1141:2;
1286:2; 1348:5; 1588:3
ἐγ, 198:35; 214:3; 742:17

306

www.ingramcontent.com/pod-product-compliance
Lightning Source LLC
Chambersburg PA
CBHW071147090426
42736CB00012B/2265